INTRODUCTION ...

This guide is designed to cover all areas of Resistant Materials including design, skills, materials, techniques and production processes. In covering the core features of all the main specifications it attempts to present the key subject matter in a visually attractive, unintimidating way. The book is meant to be used throughout the two years of study as a course guide as well as an exam revision aid and as such includes many tips on the presentation of coursework.

EDITED BY: BRIAN RUSSELL

Head of Design and Technology at Dixon's City Technology College in Bradford. Member of the Royal College of Art Schools Technology Project writing team. Principal moderator for Product Design at GCSE, and a Gatsby Teacher Fellow for Design and Technology.

Many thanks to Debbie Eason for providing many of the illustrations in this guide.

CONTENTS

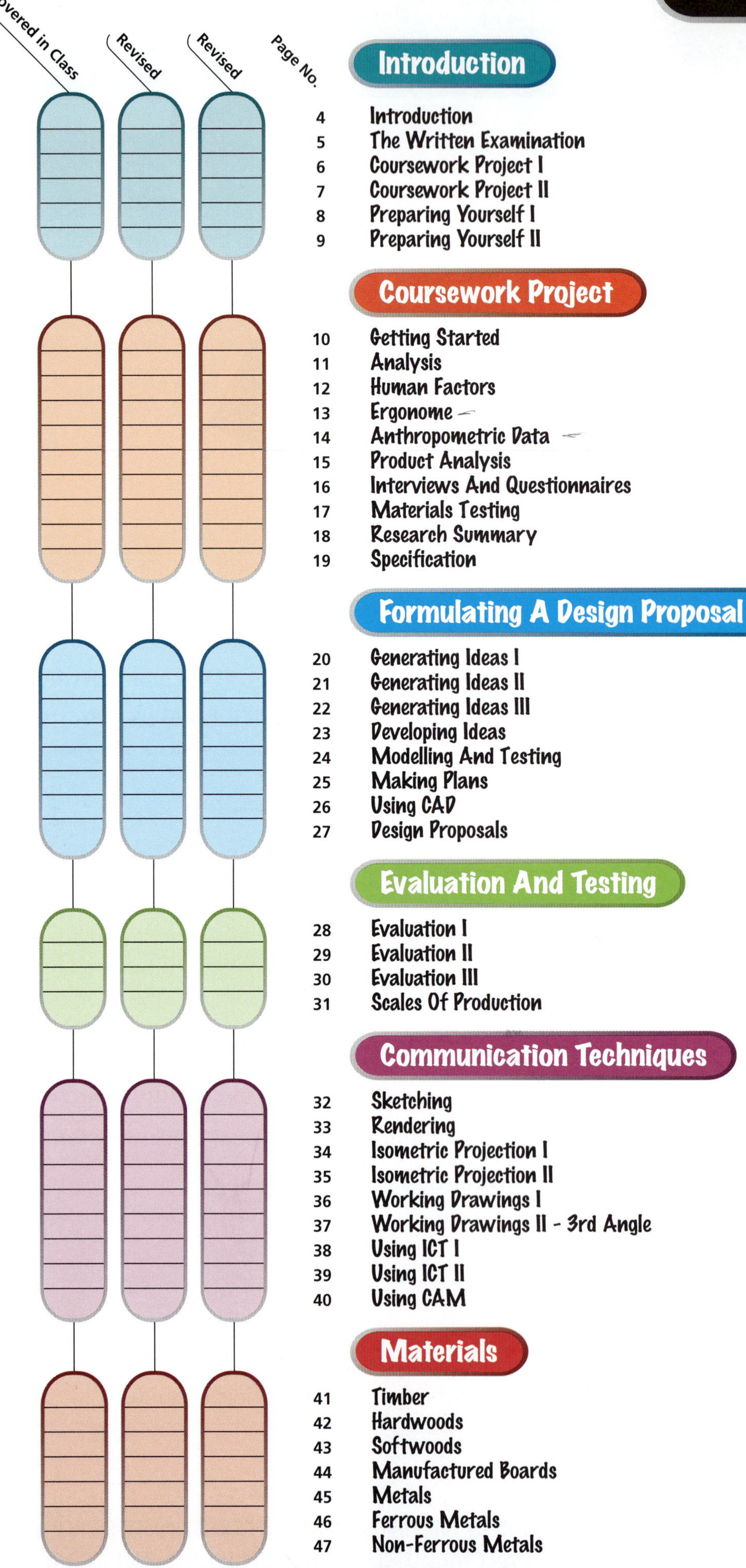

Covered in Class   Revised   Revised   Page No.

Introduction

4   Introduction
5   The Written Examination
6   Coursework Project I
7   Coursework Project II
8   Preparing Yourself I
9   Preparing Yourself II

Coursework Project

10   Getting Started
11   Analysis
12   Human Factors
13   Ergonome
14   Anthropometric Data
15   Product Analysis
16   Interviews And Questionnaires
17   Materials Testing
18   Research Summary
19   Specification

Formulating A Design Proposal

20   Generating Ideas I
21   Generating Ideas II
22   Generating Ideas III
23   Developing Ideas
24   Modelling And Testing
25   Making Plans
26   Using CAD
27   Design Proposals

Evaluation And Testing

28   Evaluation I
29   Evaluation II
30   Evaluation III
31   Scales Of Production

Communication Techniques

32   Sketching
33   Rendering
34   Isometric Projection I
35   Isometric Projection II
36   Working Drawings I
37   Working Drawings II - 3rd Angle
38   Using ICT I
39   Using ICT II
40   Using CAM

Materials

41   Timber
42   Hardwoods
43   Softwoods
44   Manufactured Boards
45   Metals
46   Ferrous Metals
47   Non-Ferrous Metals

CONTENTS

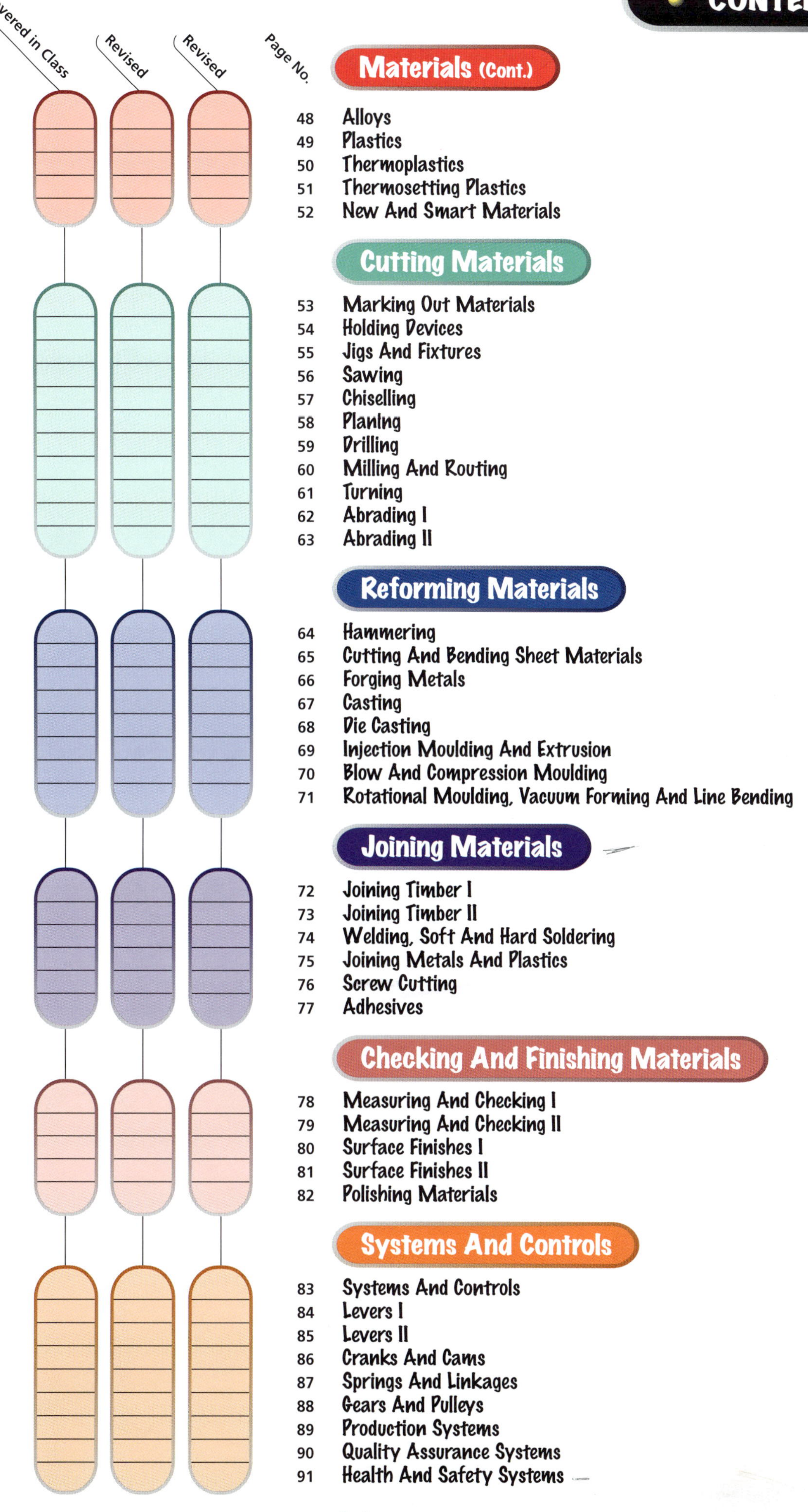

Covered in Class | Revised | Revised | Page No.

Materials (Cont.)

48 Alloys
49 Plastics
50 Thermoplastics
51 Thermosetting Plastics
52 New And Smart Materials

Cutting Materials

53 Marking Out Materials
54 Holding Devices
55 Jigs And Fixtures
56 Sawing
57 Chiselling
58 Planing
59 Drilling
60 Milling And Routing
61 Turning
62 Abrading I
63 Abrading II

Reforming Materials

64 Hammering
65 Cutting And Bending Sheet Materials
66 Forging Metals
67 Casting
68 Die Casting
69 Injection Moulding And Extrusion
70 Blow And Compression Moulding
71 Rotational Moulding, Vacuum Forming And Line Bending

Joining Materials

72 Joining Timber I
73 Joining Timber II
74 Welding, Soft And Hard Soldering
75 Joining Metals And Plastics
76 Screw Cutting
77 Adhesives

Checking And Finishing Materials

78 Measuring And Checking I
79 Measuring And Checking II
80 Surface Finishes I
81 Surface Finishes II
82 Polishing Materials

Systems And Controls

83 Systems And Controls
84 Levers I
85 Levers II
86 Cranks And Cams
87 Springs And Linkages
88 Gears And Pulleys
89 Production Systems
90 Quality Assurance Systems
91 Health And Safety Systems

92 Index

In 2000 some changes were made to the way you will be taught and tested in your GCSE courses. This book has been written taking into account those changes. Older books may use other names and terms which might make it confusing.

Examination Boards were amalgamated into larger Awarding Bodies. There are three Awarding Bodies in England:

Assessment and Qualifications Alliance usually known as AQA
Oxford Cambridge and RSA Examinations usually known as OCR
Edexcel

Each one of these has a website where you can access information about what you will be taught and how you will be assessed

www.AQA.org.uk
www.OCR.org.uk
www.Edexcel.org.uk

In addition to the English Awarding Bodies, there are separate ones for Northern Ireland and Wales.

Each of the Awarding Bodies has produced a specification for Design & Technology: Resistant Materials Technology and have to follow similar guidelines. This book will provide useful advice regardless of which Awarding Body your school is using.

A Specification contains information about what you should be taught and how you will be assessed. A specification is what used to be called a syllabus.

Ask your teacher which specification you are following.

This will take place at the end of the course and will make up **40%** of the GCSE grade. The majority of Awarding Bodies set one single paper, although you might have two. Some will provide you with a theme for part of the examination. This theme might be something like Children's Toys or Garden Furniture and will allow you to focus part of your preparation time in this area. Beware though; the papers need to test the whole specification so not everything will fit the theme.

Typically they will be about two hours in duration so you will need to prepare thoroughly for this part of the assessment.

The Examiner's Advice

It is their job to set a written examination which will test out your knowledge and understanding related to designing and making with resistant materials. As a general guide, they plan questions so they will earn you a mark a minute. If you have a ten mark question you are expected to spend about ten minutes on that question.

Ensure That You Particularly Revise The Following Areas:

Timbers – hardwoods, softwoods and manufactured boards
Metals – ferrous, non-ferrous and alloys
Plastics – Thermoplastics and thermosetting plastics
Components used for fastening materials together
Adhesives and joining methods
Ways of working materials – wastage, addition and reforming
Finishing methods
Tools and machinery for working these materials
Manufacturing processes used both in school and in industry
Mechanisms
Health & Safety issues
Wider social issues for D&T
Anthropometrics and ergonomics

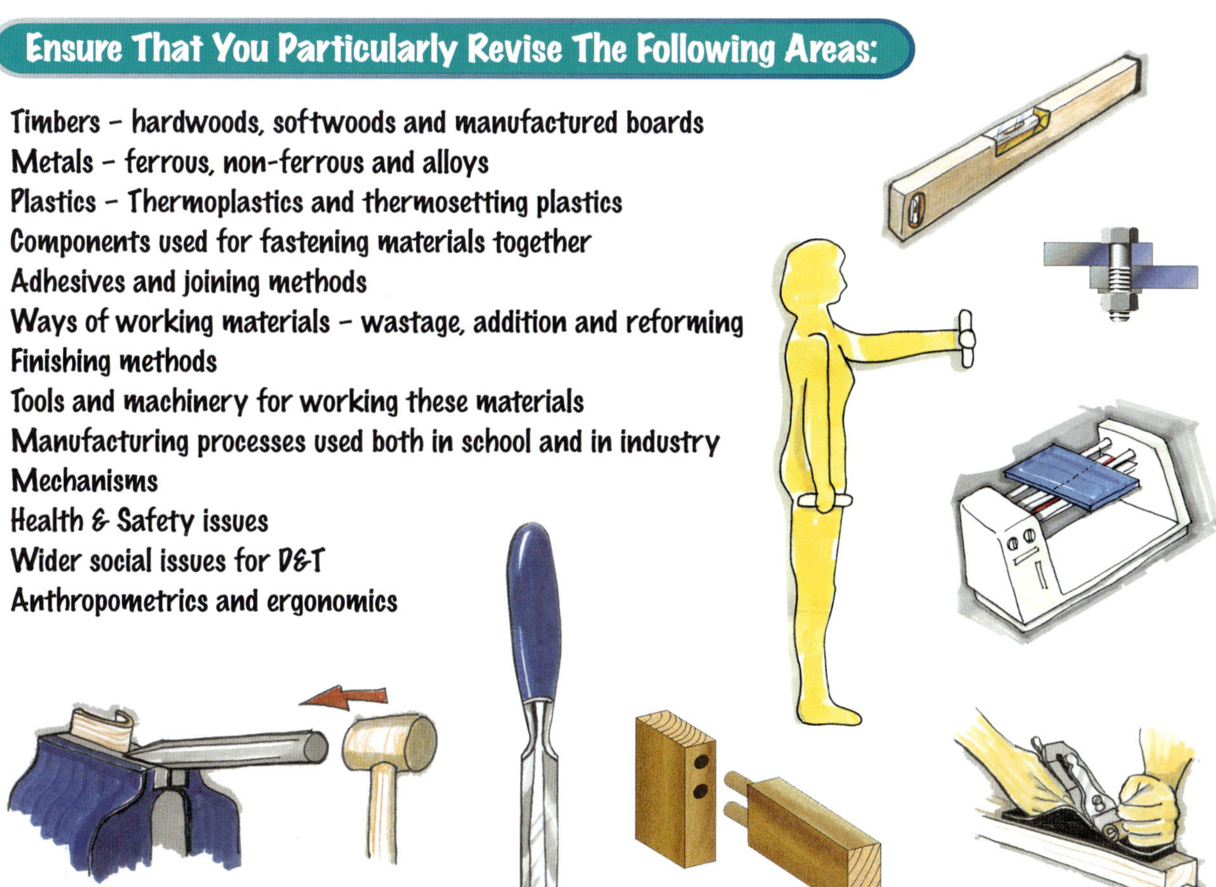

You will be required to undertake a single project which involves designing, making and testing a new product. This project is supposed to take about 40 hours of your lesson time if you are following a full GCSE and about 20 hours for a short course. It will consist of a concise design folder which explains the problem you have chosen to look into, the research you undertake, the specification for the product, the ideas you think up and how you develop them towards a final design proposal. It will also need a work-plan, which should be detailed enough for someone else to follow, the testing you do at various stages and final evaluation of the product, which should take into account how it would be commercially manufactured. You will also need to manufacture a prototype or scale model of your design.

This work will account for 60% of your final GCSE grade. It will be marked by your teacher and then seen by a moderator from the Awarding Body. The moderator might adjust your teacher's marks up or down.

The Moderator's Advice

The Principal Moderator is in charge of this part of the assessment. He or she sets a standard for each grade and checks that the moderator is assessing to the same standard. Unlike your teacher, the moderator will not have the opportunity of seeing how you progress with this project. They will not be able to talk to you or ask you questions but must make their assessment on the evidence you provide. Your design folder and the notes and drawings you provide are a vital part of the assessment process. Do not assume that the moderator understands what you are thinking; you will have to tell him through your annotation.

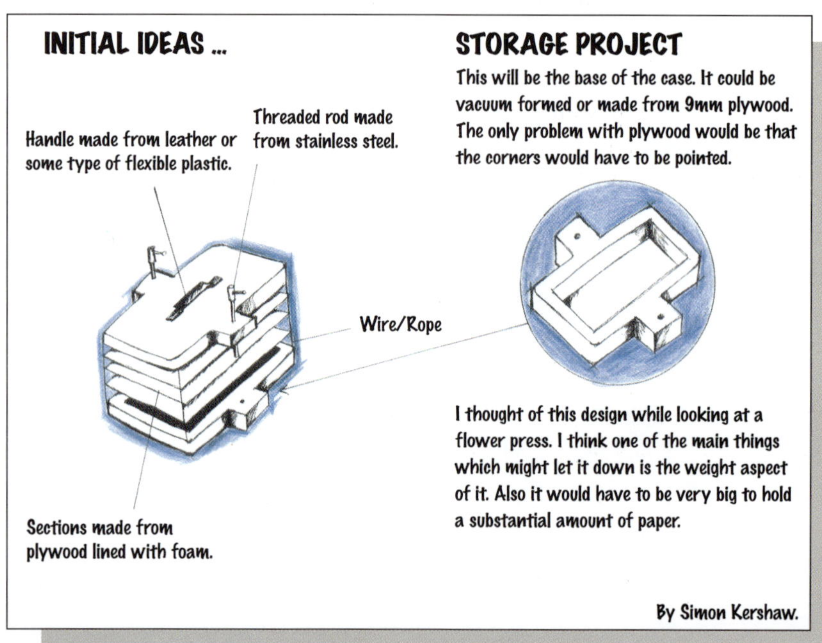

You Should Provide The Following

- A brief explanation of the project which should include a design brief
- Details of the research which you needed to undertake
- Your analysis of the problem and the research material collected
- A specification for the new product
- A range of initial ideas which meet this specification
- The development of one or more ideas
- A final design proposal and work-plan in enough detail for the moderator to follow
- Testing and evaluations throughout the design folder
- The quality assurance checks you needed to make
- How the product would be manufactured commercially

This design folder should show your industrial understanding and your ability to communicate your thinking. It is expected that you use a variety of Information and Communication Technology whenever it is appropriate to do so. You should also show your wider understanding about design and technology issues such as the environmental implications of your product.

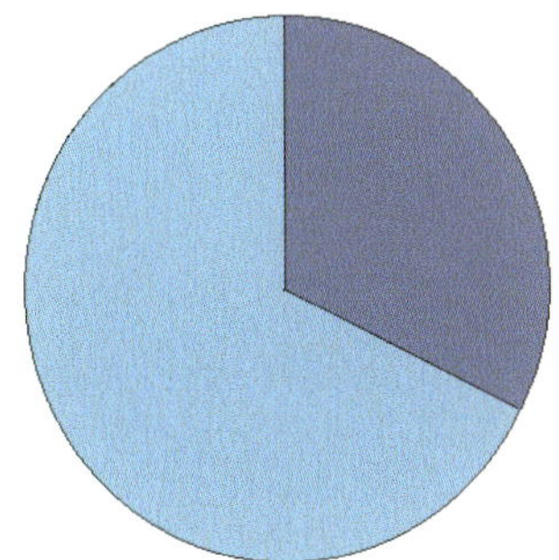

Altogether you should spend about one third of your time (about 13 hours for a full course, half this for a short course) on this part of the project. Extra marks will be awarded for the quality of your written communication so try to make sure that what you write is clear and correctly spelt.

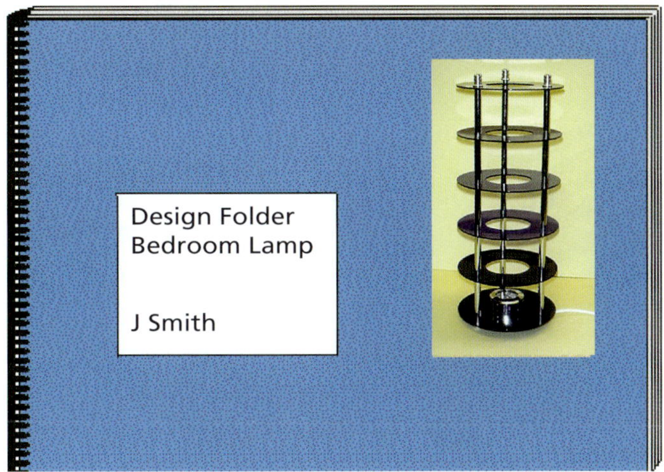

During the remaining 27 hours (half this for a short course) it is expected that you will manufacture a good quality prototype or model. Some of this time might be spent testing out construction methods and making models.

In order for you to work efficiently you will need to organize yourself with a range of resources, materials and equipment. Some are essential to you; others are luxury items which will be useful.

AN A3 DRAWING BOARD AND T-SQUARE

An A3 drawing board is not essential but will make your life easier. What is essential is a smooth drawing surface.

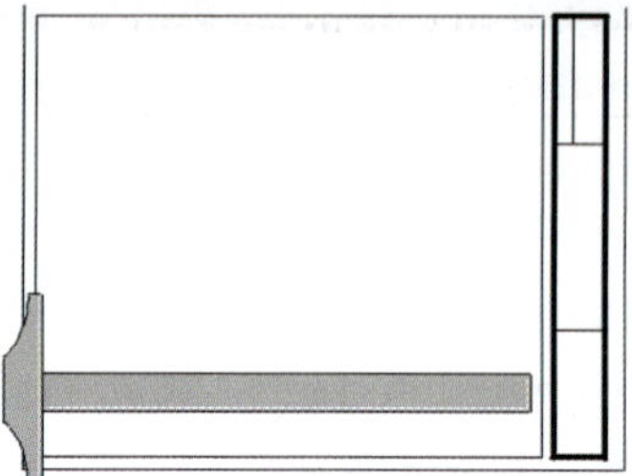

SET SQUARES

Used in conjunction with a drawing board to draw accurate angles. The 60°/30° set square is used for isometric projection.

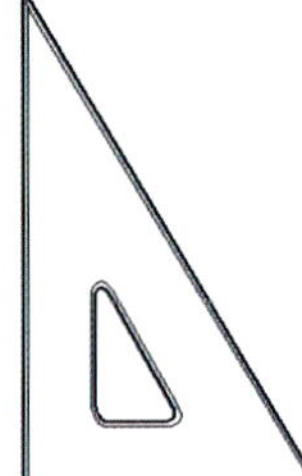

300mm RULER/PROTRACTOR

Rulers are used for measuring widths and thicknesses and act as a guide to drawing isometric projections. The protractor is used to measure angles.

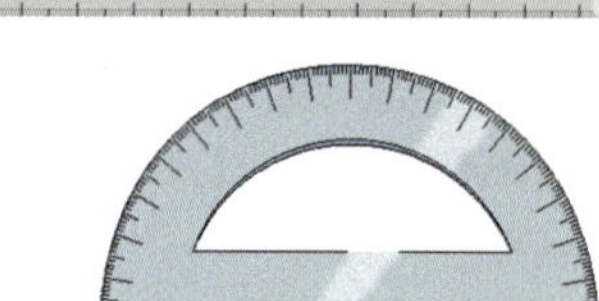

GRAPHITE PENCILS

HB and 2B would be useful for shading.
2H would be useful for construction lines

COLOURED PENCILS

A range of good quality coloured pencils are a sound investment

ERASER

A good quality eraser will remove your mistakes with less fuss

FINELINE PEN

A low-cost fineline pen is essential for enhancing your drawings

FELT TIP PENS

Less useful than coloured pencils. Primary colours and shades of grey are most useful

PAIR OF COMPASSES

Used to draw accurate circles/arcs

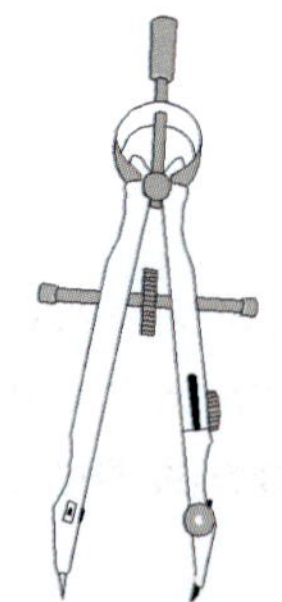

CAMERA

A camera is especially useful when undertaking primary research and recording your modelling.

ELLIPSE TEMPLATES

Make drawing circles in isometric projection much easier.

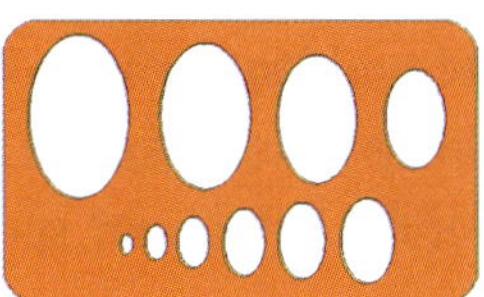

CIRCLE TEMPLATES

Make drawing smaller circles much easier than using a pair of compasses.

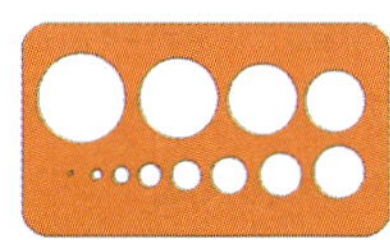

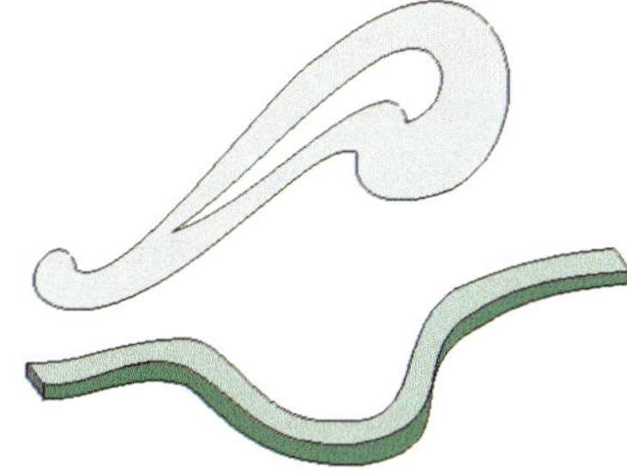

TAPE MEASURE

Essential for helping to finalise larger dimensions.

FRENCH CURVES / FLEXIBLE CURVES

For producing smooth lines on curved parts of a drawing.

PORTFOLIO CASE

Essential for keeping your design work together. The type with ten pockets is especially useful as it will help you to focus on producing a concise design folder with a maximum of twenty sheets.

COMPUTER

With appropriate software such as Corel Draw!, 2D Design Tools, Pro/DESKTOP etc. could make some of your design tasks much easier. Check with your school, they might have software licenses which allow you to have copies for use at home.

Remember, to work effectively at home you need a quiet area and space to spread out your work and equipment. Do not do your homework whilst sitting in front of the television, it will take you much longer!

The following sections take you through the coursework project in some detail. You might find it useful to follow a similar design method with all of the designing and making during your GCSE course. The design folder does need to be a concise document which shows your thinking. As a general guide, twenty A3 sheets should be ample for most projects. You will need to organise this carefully but do not spend too much time drawing elaborate borders and titles. Content is what gains you marks.

How Should I Start My Project?

You need to begin by explaining the problem you hope to solve through your designing and making. One way of doing this is to clearly explain the market need you are designing for. Remember that you need to assume that the product you design will be commercially manufactured.

Try to explain:
- the type of people who would use your product.
- the environment the product would be designed for.
- any cost constraints which would influence your design.

Designing for a real client will often mean that you undertake real primary research and this will provide you with much more useful evaluations at each stage.

Managing your time is really important. 40 hours is not very long, make every minute count.

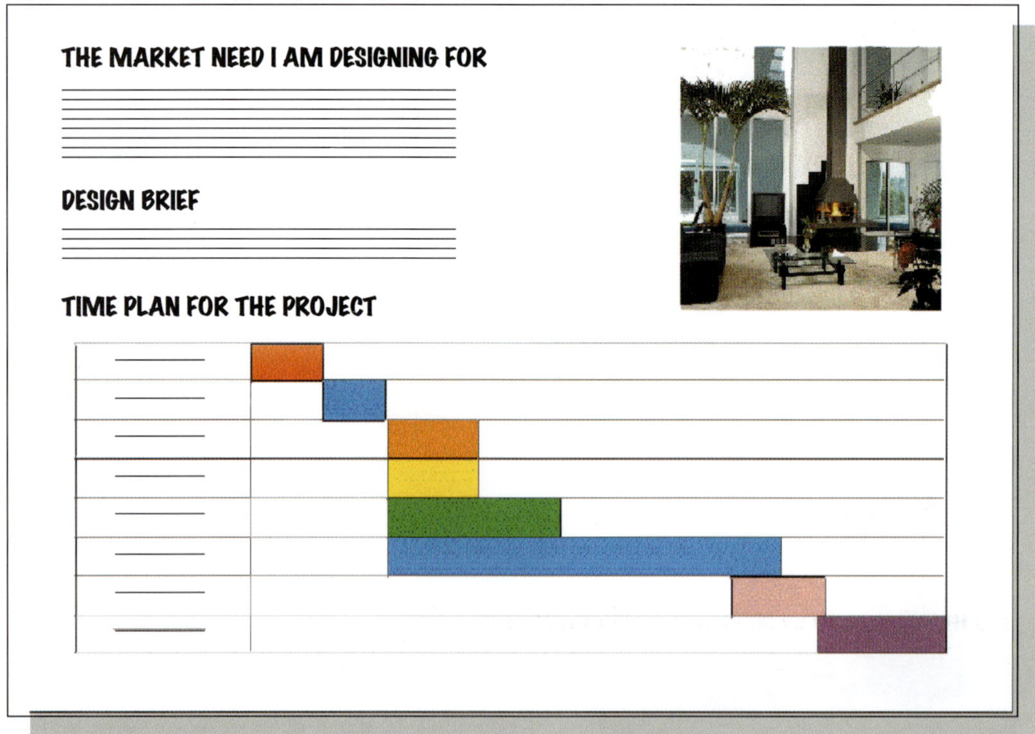

It is useful to work out a time-plan for your project with your teacher. Students often spend too much time on one part of the work. A time-plan should help you to manage your time. Remember, only one third of your project should be designing, the rest of the time should be spent working with materials.

You will need to consider the problem in more detail and organise your first thoughts. One way you can do this is by brainstorming under the four headings: People, Places, Products and Processes. This is often called the '4P's method'.

People

List all of the people you might need to talk to. Do you need to conduct interviews or construct questionnaires? Do you need expert advice? You might need to use the telephone or e-mail to contact people. Letters rarely get good results and can waste a lot of time.

Places

List all of the places you might need to visit. The library might be one useful starting point. A visit to relevant shops or a visit to the actual environment you are designing for would be sensible. Will you need to visit a factory or a DIY warehouse? Do you need to take measurements of environments?

Products

List all of the similar products you may need to look at. Remember that products designed for one purpose can often provide ideas for a new product. Product analysis is probably the most useful form of research you can undertake. You might consider looking at the work of famous designers or the influence of design movements such as Art Deco.

Processes

List all of the materials and processes you might need to investigate. This is the hardest section to complete at this stage. If a key requirement of your product is for it to be adjustable then an investigation into mechanisms might be a good starting point. Work under this heading will often turn into practical investigations.

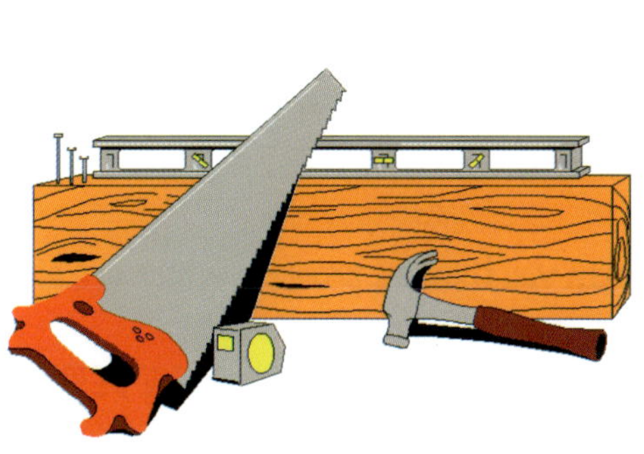

You might need to do some practical experiments with materials and processes.

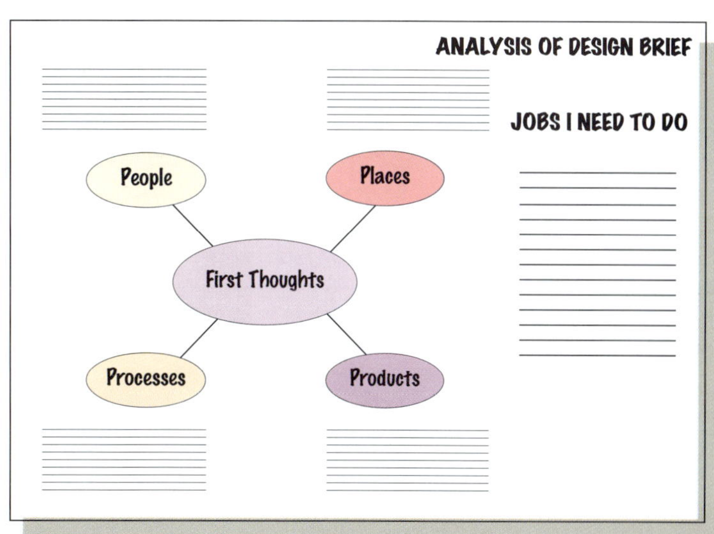

Ideally, you should list all of the tasks you will need to undertake during the project. Remember that you have been studying Design & Technology for several years and you already know a great deal. Can you list what you already know that is relevant to this product?

Most products are designed for humans therefore you will need to consider Human Factors. If you are designing entirely for animals then a similar investigation might be needed although you may find information harder to come by.

Anthropometrics

Anthropometrics is the study of human measurements. Measurements have been taken from millions of people of all shapes and sizes and put together in charts. Designers try to work to the 5th - 95th percentile. That means that 90% of the population are catered for. However, if there are all those measurements to choose from which ones do you use? Think about it. If you are designing a doorway you would choose the tallest. If you are designing a seat then the shortest might be the best compromise. There are lots of specific books and websites which deal with this in more detail.

Ergonomics

Ergonomics is the study of efficiency of people in their working environment and often deals with the application of anthropometric data. Ergonomics deals with issues such as comfort and safety. What colour is best for safety equipment? How much weight can one person safely lift?

Inclusive Design

The ideal product is one that meets everyone's needs. Called 'inclusive design' it is an impossible aim but we should perhaps try to exclude as few people as possible. Physical ability, health, intellectual ability etc. are all human factors which designers need to consider.

Stereotypes

Not everyone is the same. However people are often put into different groups. These stereotypes can be useful to designers, manufacturers and especially retailers. Ensuring that products are aimed at particular market groups is common practice.

Can you think of products which are aimed at specific groups?
This is often called EXCLUSIVE DESIGN.

And Finally ...

You should explain what human factors you will need to consider. You may need to conduct your own research if the information is not readily available. It might be worth making yourself an ergonome from cardboard so you can test out your drawings.

ERGONOME

Photocopy this page onto a sheet of thin card. Cut out the body parts with scissors and join with brass paper fasteners to make an ergonome.

This can be useful when designing furniture products, for example.

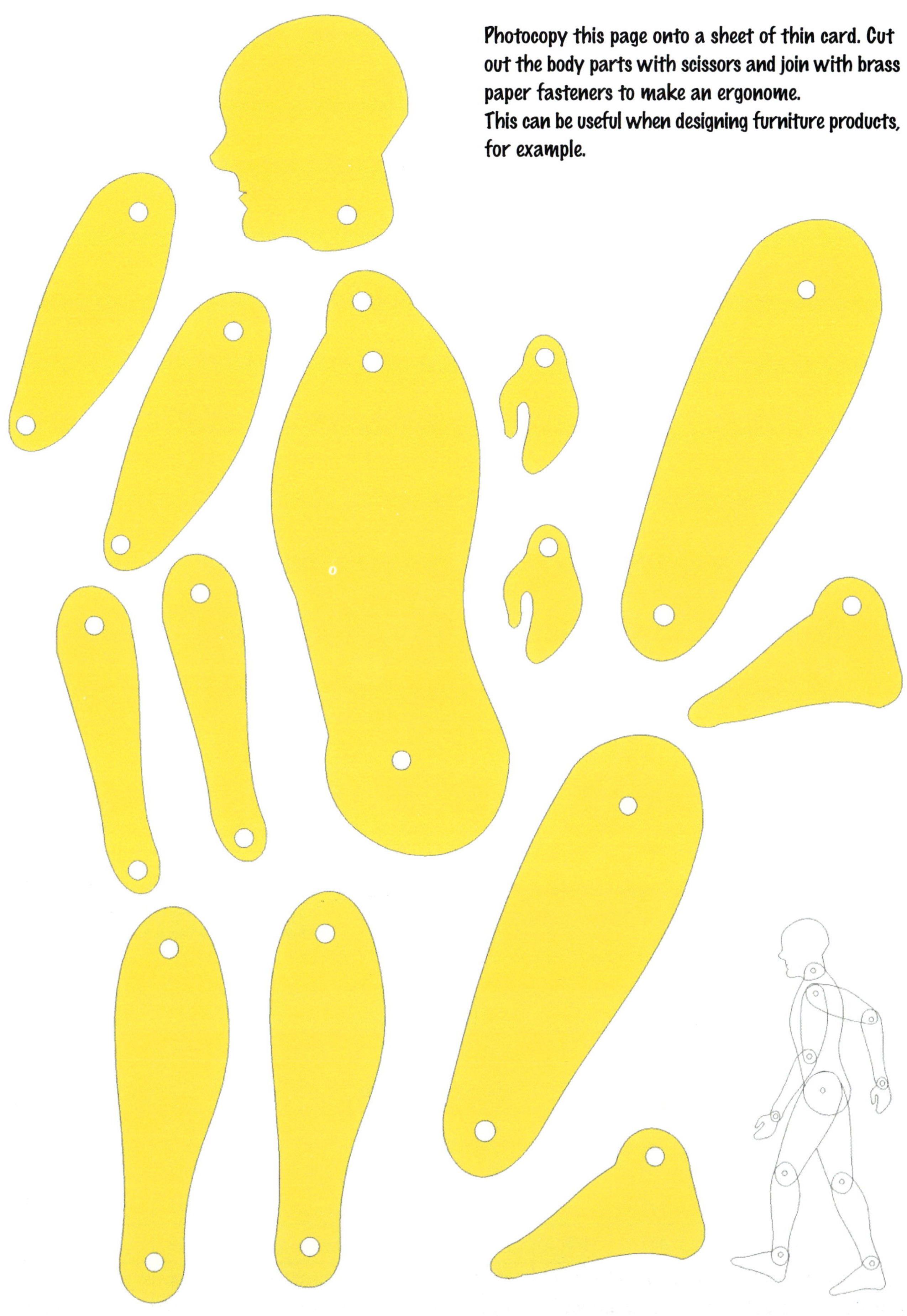

Here is an example of data for the sitting and standing positions. This could be used for reference in your coursework. More detailed data may be found in your local library.

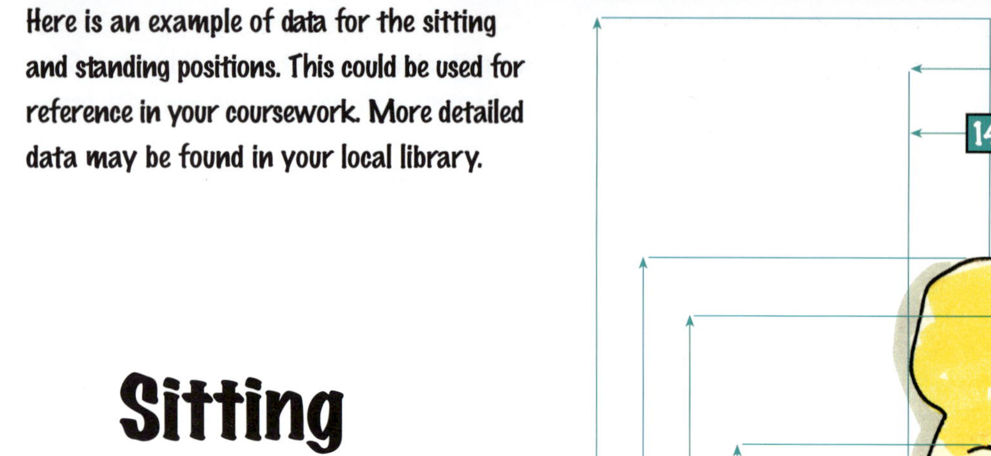

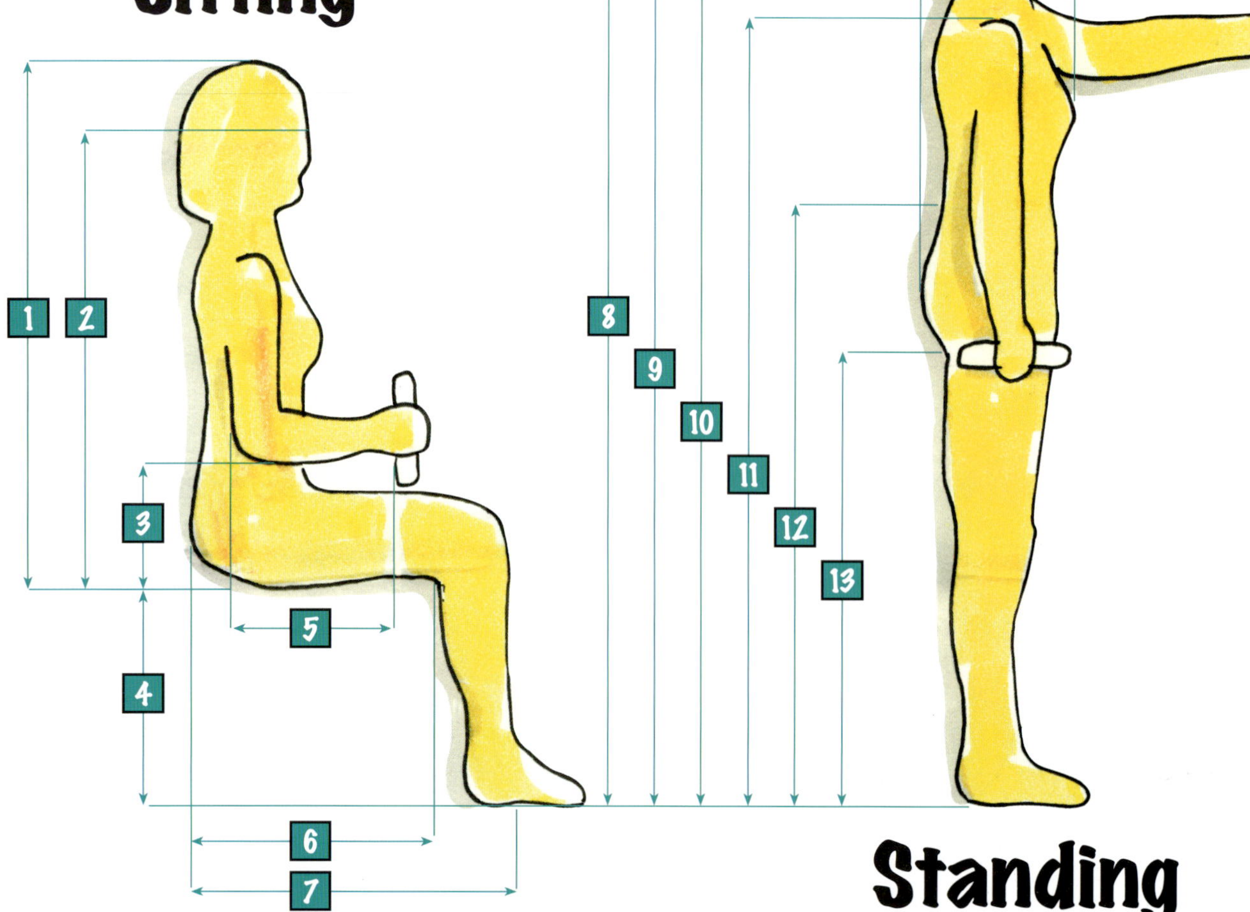

	SITTING	SHORT	AVERAGE	TALL
1	Sitting height	795	880	965
2	Sitting eye height	685	765	845
3	Sitting elbow height	185	240	295
4	Popliteal height	355	420	490
5	Elbow-grip length	304	343	387
6	Buttock-popliteal length	435	488	550
7	Buttock-knee length	520	583	645
	BODY WEIGHT	44.1kg	68.5kg	93.7kg

	STANDING	SHORT	AVERAGE	TALL
8	Vertical grip reach	1790	1983	2190
9	Stature	1505	1675	1855
10	Eye height	1405	1568	1745
11	Shoulder height	1215	1368	1535
12	Elbow height	930	1048	1180
13	Knuckle height	660	738	825
14	Chest depth	210	250	285
15	Forward grip reach	650	743	835

These tables give a range of data from smallest to largest sizes. __ALL MEASUREMENTS ARE IN MILLIMETRES.__

Product analysis is probably the most useful research you can undertake. It involves looking carefully at a product, taking it apart (or imagining taking it apart) and working out how it was made.

How To Analyse A Product

Materials What materials have been used and why? Can you identify and list the characteristics of the materials used in each component.

Function What is the need for the product? What was the target market it was aimed at? What is it designed to do? How does it work? Can it be maintained easily?

Ergonomics Has the product been designed to make it safer, easier and more efficient to use? Are there any ways in which these characteristics could be improved? How easy is it to lift and carry? How easy is it to assemble?

Manufacturing How was it made? Can you identify the process which was used for each component?

Style How can you describe the style? Is it modern? Has it been influenced by a design movement?

Other Factors

You are expected to consider the wider implications of designing and manufacturing. This is a good place in your folder to show that you have done so. Can the product be recycled? What does its life cycle look like? What has been the effect of this product on our lifestyles? Is a particular group of people excluded from using the product?

Seeking opinions and ideas from other people is an essential tool of the designer.

Interviews

Interviews are one of the best ways of gaining information from people. Prepare the questions in advance and make sure you record the responses. A Dictaphone or small cassette recorder is the best way of doing this although you might consider getting a friend to take notes.

Questionnaires

Writing questionnaires is a skill all of its own. It can be time consuming and can often prove to be unhelpful in moving you forward. It is the analysis of the data not the data collection which the moderator is looking for.

Consider:
• writing a group questionnaire (on teenage trends for example) and sharing the results.
• using data collected by a commercial organisation (such as a teenager's magazine).
• writing a single questionnaire and using it as the basis for conducting interviews.

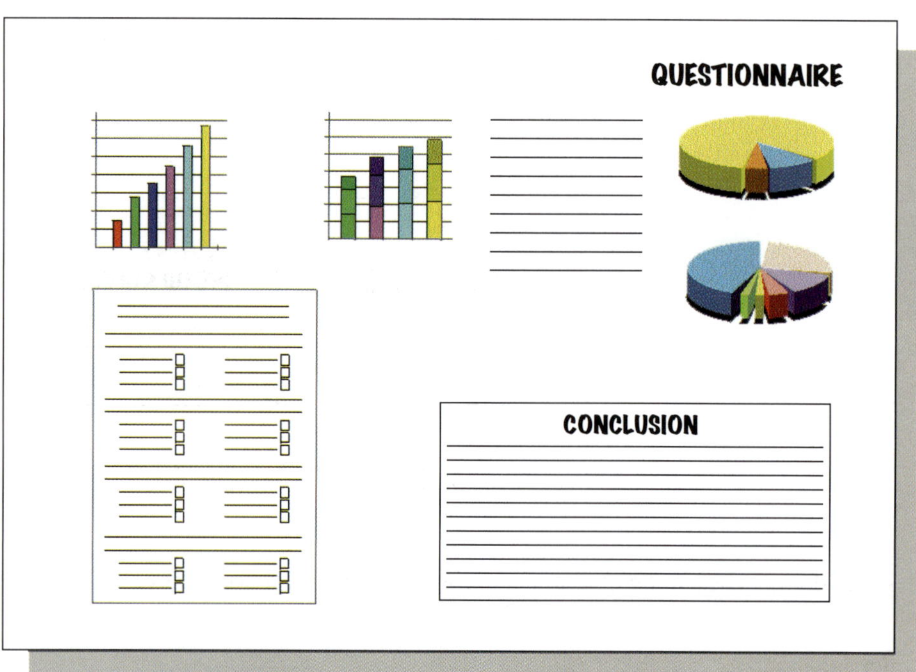

Databases or spreadsheets can help you collate the results of your questionnaire and can generate useful graphs. It is essential to explain how the survey was carried out, what questions were asked and how the results influence your thinking.

Remember, asking ten people is unlikely to provide you with a valid survey result. You need to target your potential users and seek a good cross-section of opinions if your data is to be reliable.

Genuine materials testing can provide some useful information to help you with your designing, especially at the development stage. However, it does need to be your own testing to gain you credit.

How To Set About Testing Materials

There are many databases and CD-ROMS which can do this work for you but moderators hate reading sheets full of copied material and tend to ignore this work. This is just as true if it has been copied from books or downloaded from the Internet.

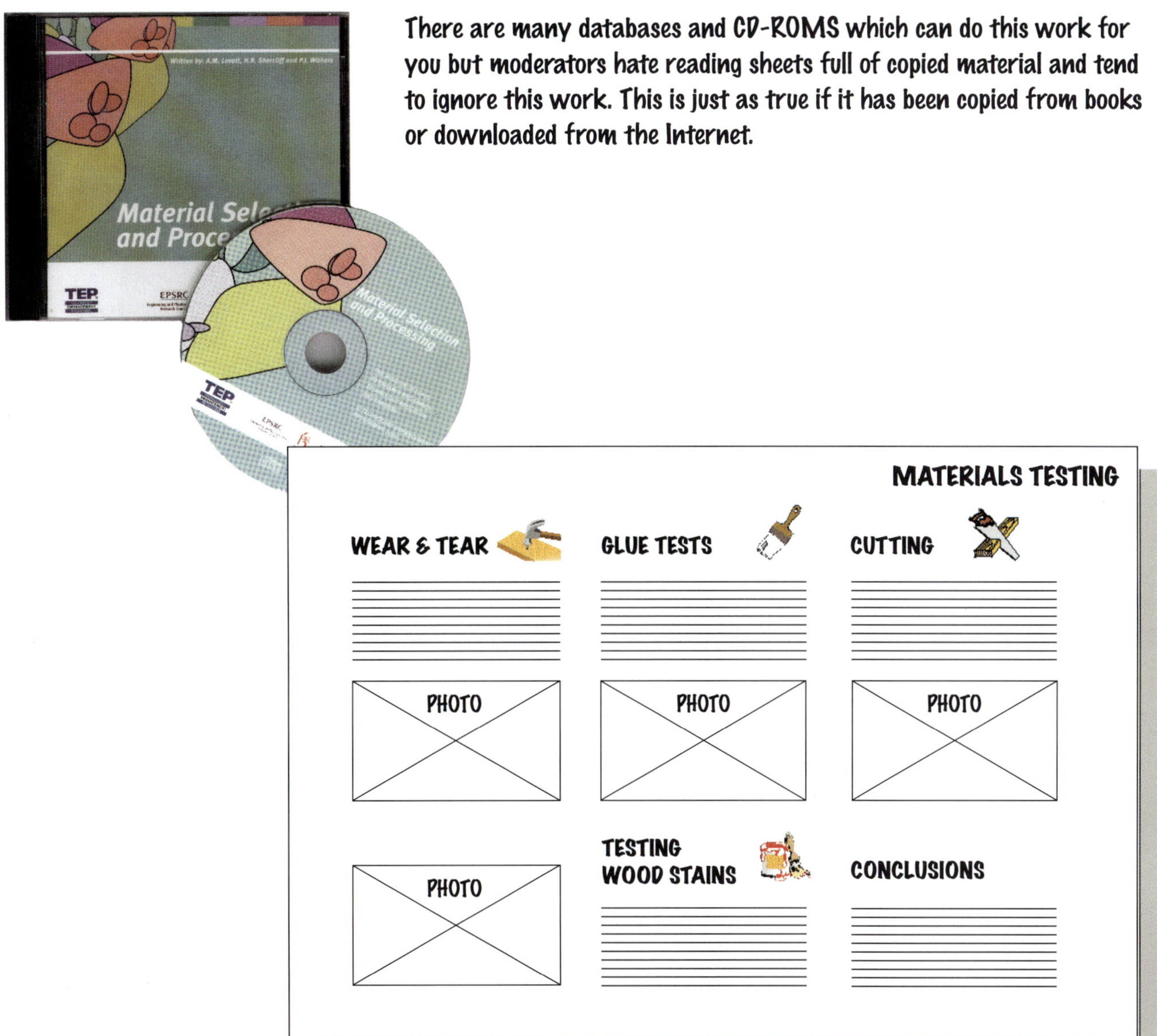

Tests do not need to be complex; they need to be useful and make fair comparisons between materials.

Consider testing:
- different finishes on thin samples of materials.
- a variety of glues.
- how materials and finishes stand up to knocks and scratches.
- whether materials float or sink or absorb water.
- how easy materials are to cut and shape.

Photographs of your tests alongside the description of how they were undertaken would be really useful. Ensure that you draw conclusions from these tests. What decisions can you now make?

The moderator does need to understand what research you have undertaken and how useful it has been. You do not need to photocopy every book page you have read or include every catalogue or leaflet you have used. A summary will do.

Summarising Your Research

Keep a list of all the books, leaflets, websites and other resources you have used during your project. Remember that additional research is often needed at the development stage where you may need to search for handles, hinges etc. or choose colours from an existing range of paints.

Primary research, such as conducting interviews or analysing products, will gain you far more credit than secondary research based on reading books or Internet searches.

Bullet point your research summary or produce a chart so you can list the material as your work progresses.

SUMMARY RESEARCH

SOURCE	WHAT I FOUND	HOW IT HELPED ME

SUMMARY OF RESEARCH

- _______________
- _______________
- _______________
- _______________
- _______________
- _______________

Your specification should provide a detailed description of what the product is to be. It should reflect information found in your research and a third party should be able to use your specification to start to plan and develop ideas which would result in a final product. A specification is often best displayed as a bullet point list.

- **Target market** Who is the target market? Having conducted research do you need to revise what you wrote on your first sheet?

- **Function** What does your product need to do?

- **Size** Are there any restrictions? Can you specify a size at this stage?

- **Weight** Is this important? How will the customer transport it home?

- **Durability** How long do you expect your product to last? Will there be any maintenance issues, such as the need to replace batteries?

- **Aesthetics** Does your product need to match a particular style? Consider colour, form, proportion, pattern and texture.

- **Materials** What type of materials do you think are most appropriate? Do they need to have specific characteristics such as being fireproof, waterproof, easy to clean, strong, flexible etc.?

- **Safety** The British Standards Institute produces guidelines for many products. Check out their website on http://www.bsi.org.uk/education

- **Cost** Is there a limit on your budget? Does your product need to compete on price with similar products?

- **Green issues** How environmentally friendly will your product need to be?

- **Manufacture** Does your product need to use specific processes? What scale of production are you expecting your product to be manufactured on?

- **Packaging** Does your product need to pack flat? Do you need to include assembly instructions or guidance for its use?

Testing

You might need to consider how you will test your product. In industry, this forms a very important part of the specification. For example, if the product must conform to certain standards then there are specific tests that must be carried out.

SPECIFICATION

New ideas do not appear like magic, you need to make them happen. Here are a few techniques which might help you start those initial ideas flowing.

Drawing Through A Window

This is especially good for decorative products such as jewellery. Select items of interest - nature is an ideal source. This involves using a drawing template to focus on only part of an object. This can produce some interesting patterns.

A new idea for a clock face or the top of a box?

In The Style Of ...

Retro styling is very popular. Designing in the style of past design movements is a great starting point. Check out Bauhaus, Art Deco, Art Nouveau, De Stijl, Memphis, Shaker. This idea for a lamp came from looking at the Hoover Building - a famous piece of Art Deco architecture.

Setting Rules

Limiting yourself to a set of rules can sometimes mean that you produce fresh ideas that you would never have thought up without them. Try this set of rules. You can only use a maximum of three circular holes and two straight saw cuts taken from a selection of paper off-cuts.

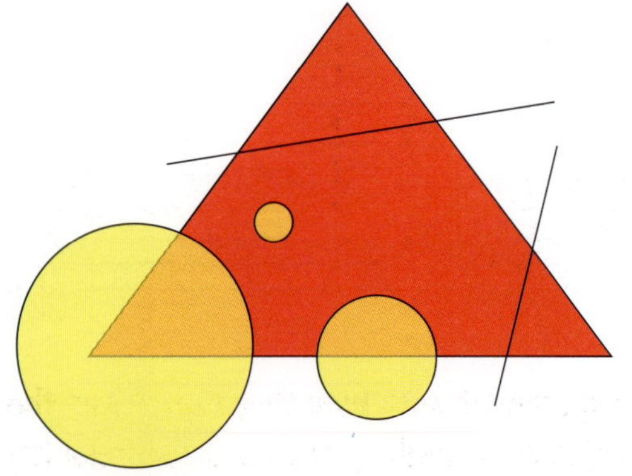
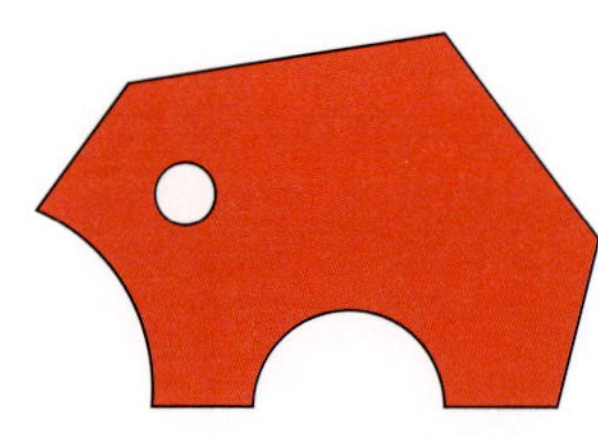

Using these rules a set of easy-to-make animals were produced for a child's toy

Looking At The Work Of Famous Designers

There are many designers from past times or the present who are inspirational to other designers. Check out Charles Rennie Mackintosh, Phillipe Starck, James Dyson, Frank Lloyd Wright, and Ettore Sottsass for starters.

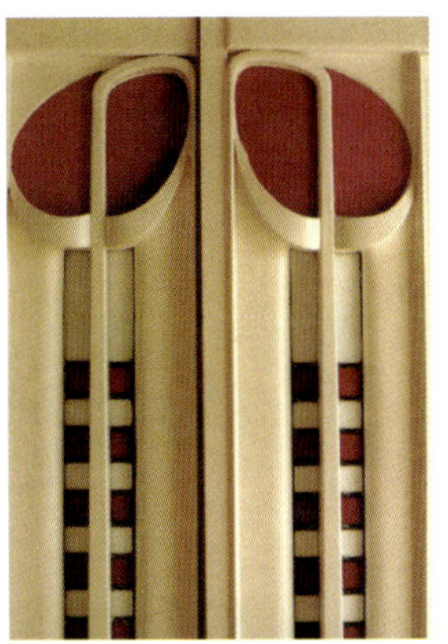

The modern silver pendant was inspired by this door decoration designed by Mackintosh in 1903.

Using Modelling

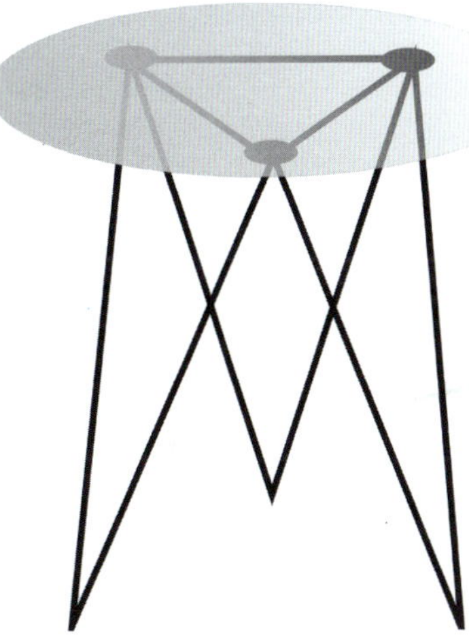

Working in 3D will often produce very different ideas from simply sitting with paper and pencil. Try one of these techniques to design a piece of furniture:

- Use only art straws and card
- Cut and fold from a single sheet of card
- Use plasticine and card
- Use wire and scraps of fabric

This modern table design came from modelling with art straws.

Working With Grids

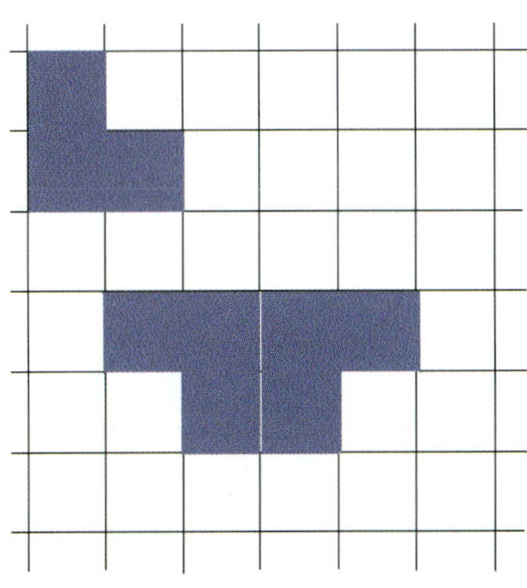

Use squared paper and cut out identical shapes from coloured paper. Experiment with how they repeat and the patterns which can be made. Scope for modular furniture? A storage system? Jewellery or a constructional toy?

Presenting Ideas

Whatever method you choose for generating your ideas you will need to present them for the moderator to see. The best ideas sheets are busy with lots of drawings and notes. You might paste ideas from several sheets together to make an interesting arrangement. If you draw with a fine-liner or ballpoint pen you can easily photocopy a pasted-up sheet. You could add some colour or tone to enhance your drawings but that is not really important at the moment.

If you have used modelling to generate ideas you will either need to draw these or photograph them. A digital camera is probably best for this if you have access to one.

Don't worry about how good your drawings are at this stage; it is the variety and feasibility of the ideas which is important. Adding notes will help you to explain your thinking to the moderator.

What Do I Write?

Start by indicating what materials you think could be used for each idea. How would they be cut and shaped? How would they be joined together?

It will be important to evaluate your ideas against your design specification. Do any of them have major weaknesses?

How Many Ideas Do I Need?

There is no real answer to this question. Between five and ten basic ideas are plenty. Maybe you can think of only one or two. If that is the case then the next stage is even more important.

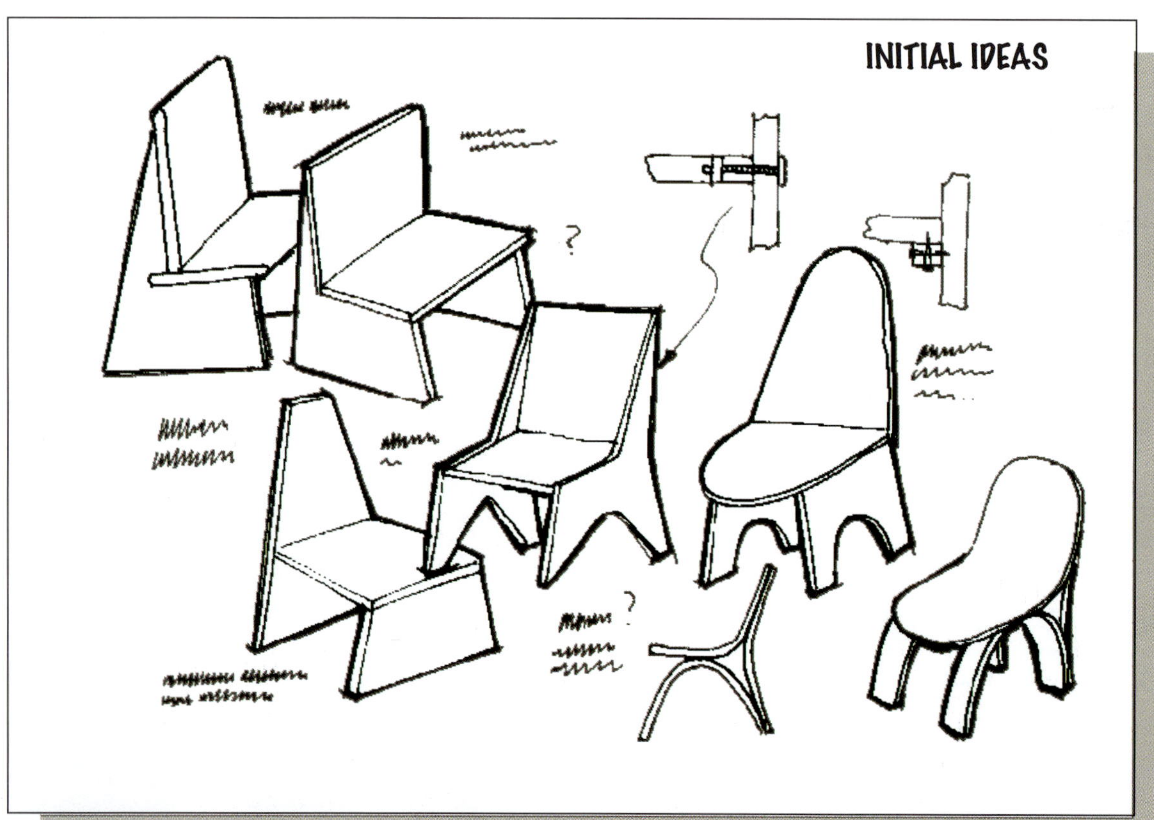

You might have two or more sheets of initial ideas but keep an eye on the time. You need to move towards the manufacturing of your chosen idea.

The moderator will need to see why you chose a particular idea to develop. You will need to explain this by evaluating the initial ideas and checking that your chosen idea satisfies your design specification.

How Do I Develop My Ideas?

One method you can try is to draw your chosen idea onto a new sheet. Then draw it again and make just one change. Draw the second design again and make one further change. It will start to evolve into a sheet full of drawings.

How Much Detail Do I Need To Show?

You will soon need to present your design in a form that someone else can follow and make. You will certainly need to present your ideas to your teacher who might give you some advice on manufacturing. Be prepared to make big changes to your idea and even go back a stage if necessary. Your teacher will have far more manufacturing experience and may well spot areas which will cause you problems later. Listen to your teacher and respond to the advice given!

Other People's Opinions

Now is a good time to seek other people's opinions, especially if you consulted them at the research stage. Make a note of any changes they suggest.

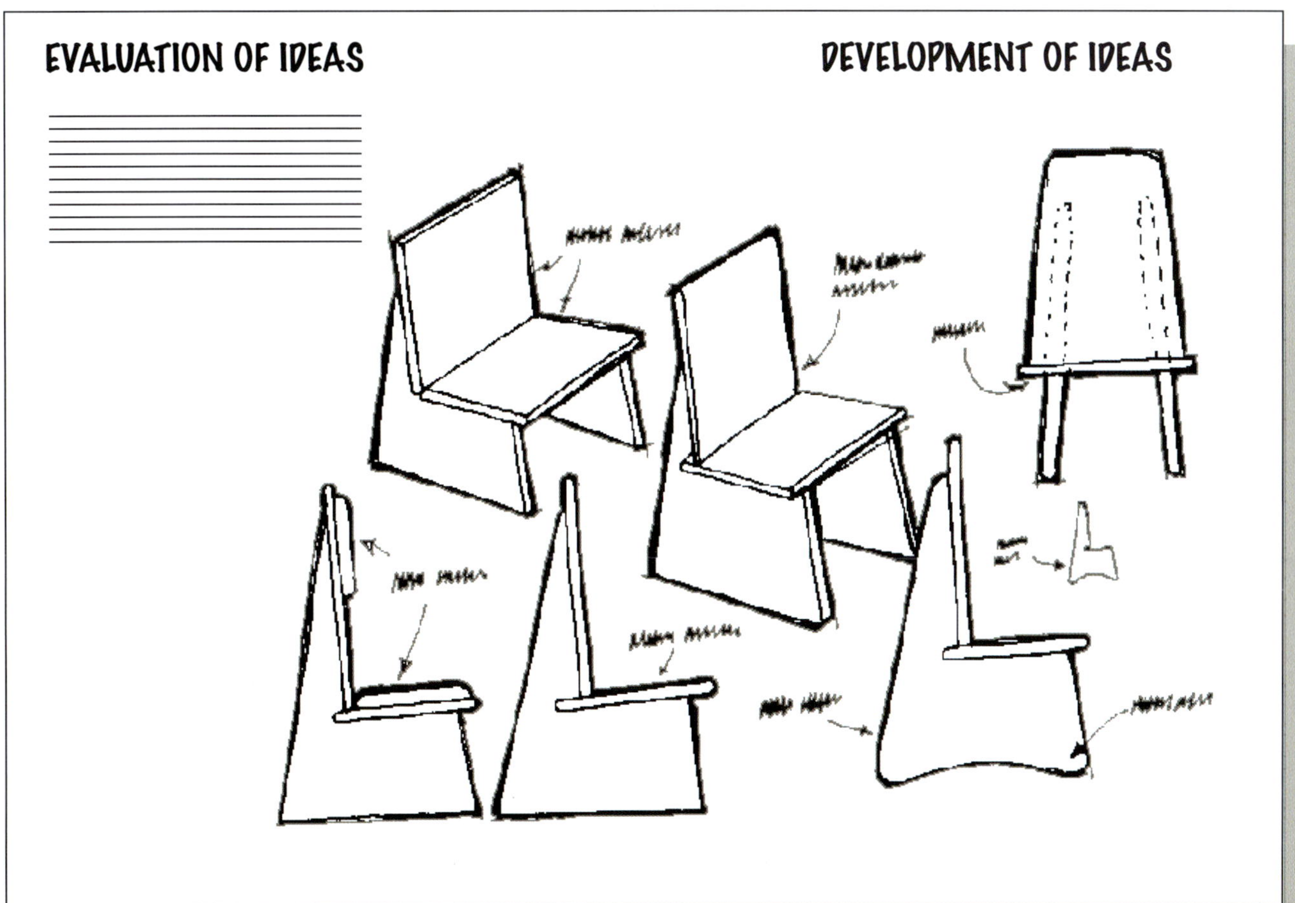

Modelling Your Best Idea

Making a good scale model at this stage can help you finalise your construction details. You might need to test out some of the construction methods full size. Card, 3mm MDF, wire etc. are often the most suitable materials to model with.

What Scale Should I Use?

That very much depends on the product you are designing. Furniture is often modelled full size using corrugated card. Rolled up newspapers and self-adhesive tape will allow frame structures to be tested.

Testing

Tests do not have to be complex, they have to be sensible. Can you finalise:

- the dimensions for your design?
- the construction methods?
- the materials you will use?
- these details with the potential user?

Be prepared to move back a stage if you discover problems with your design

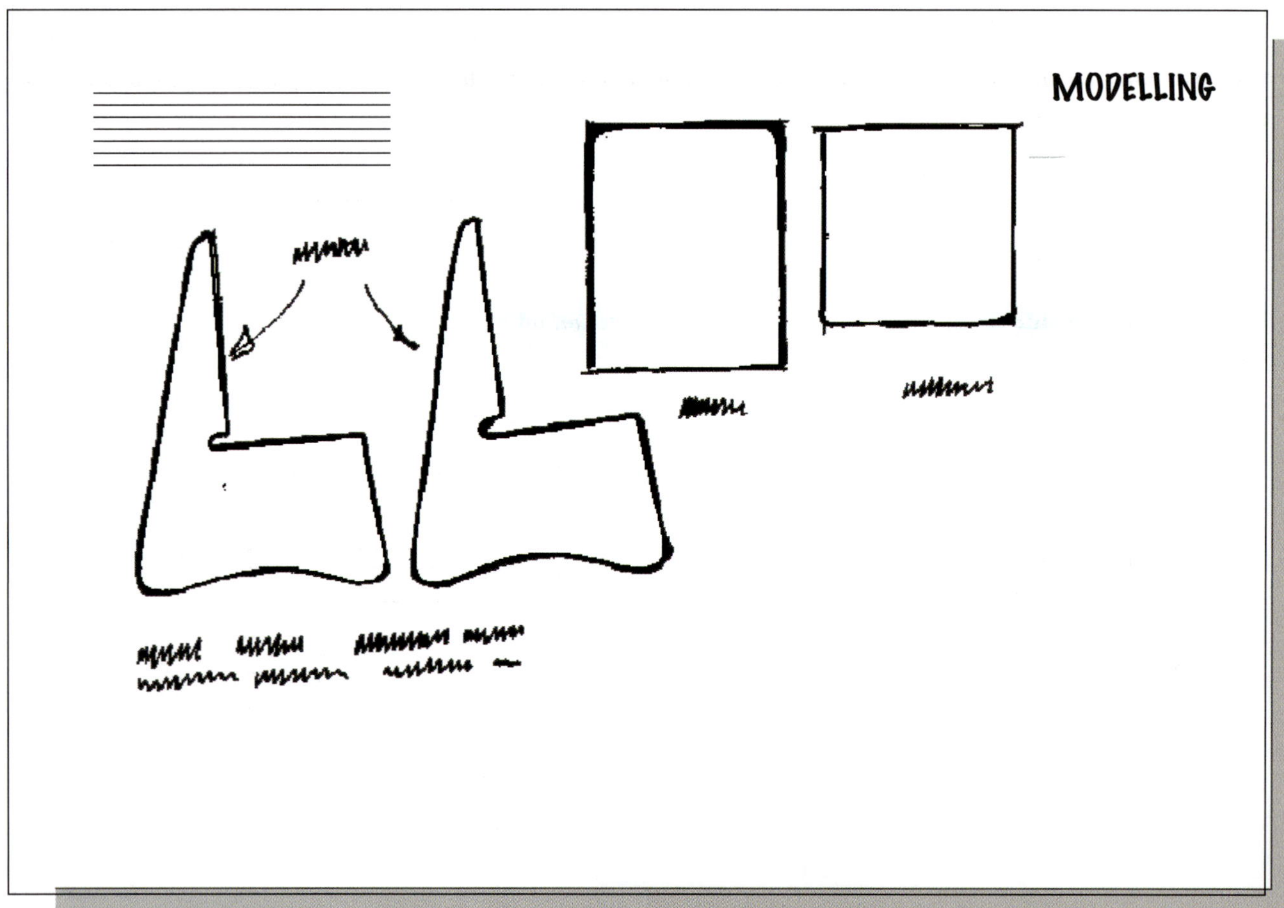

Recording this stage is very important. Explain how you went about modelling and testing your design. Use photographs to ensure the moderator can see the work you have done as models often do not last long in a workshop environment.

Your plans will vary enormously depending upon the actual project undertaken. They would be used together with drawings and/or models. The best way of presenting this information is to use a flow chart.

Flow Chart Symbols

A flow chart shows the order in which a series of tasks are carried out, in other words the sequence of events in which something is produced. There are different, specific symbols for each stage of the process. Some of these are shown below.

TERMINATOR
represents start, restart, stop.

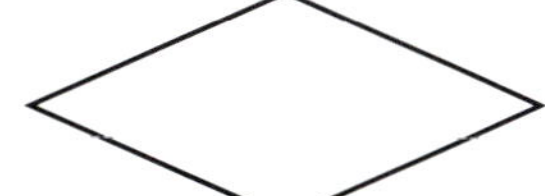

DECISION
represents a choice which can lead to another pathway.

PROCESS
represents a particular instruction or action.

INPUT/OUTPUT
represents additions to or removals from the particular process.

The symbols are linked together by arrows which indicate the correct sequence of events. The aim should be to make the flow chart as clear and simple as possible.

An Example Of A Flow Chart

This example shows how a production plan for one component may look. Always start with the correct symbol. Show each stage in a rectangle using clear easy to follow instructions. You will need to undertake some quality checks, what will they be? Quality checks require a decision so a diamond shape is used. You will need to build in feedback loops if something is found to be wrong. This would take you back one or several stages so that some process can be adjusted before going forward again.

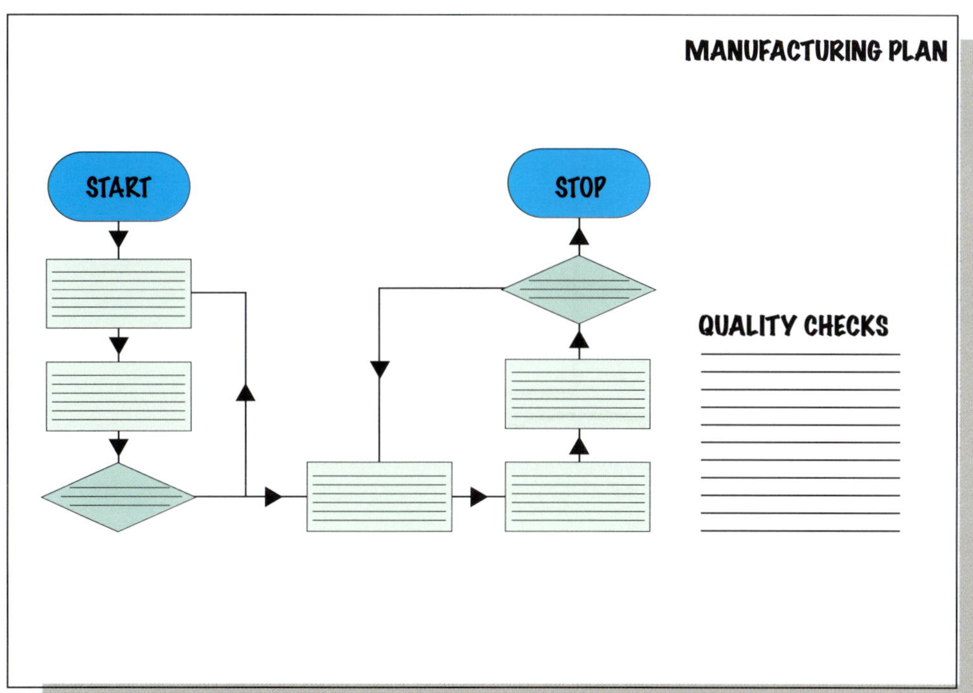

Don't use drawings, especially clipart to illustrate your plans. It is not the way industry would do it!

You could include digital photos to illustrate some complex operations. This technique is sometimes used in industry, especially when there are language difficulties.

Computer Aided Design

Computer Aided Design is being used more and more in coursework projects. If at all possible you should try to use some CAD for at least part of your final design.

Designers rarely use computers for designing in the early stages of their work, a pen or pencil is much quicker and often considered to be more creative. At the development stage however it is an essential tool in most design areas.

Electronic Product Definition

This is an industrial term and simply means that every aspect of a product is put onto a computer. This allows a range of people to work on the product at the same time. For example, engineers can analyse and test out the structure, the production team can begin to plan the tooling and the finance department can sort out how much it is all going to cost.

Using CAD In Your Project

You might use CAD to:
- make templates to draw around onto the materials you plan to cut out.
- improve the accuracy and clarity of your drawings.
- create the numerical data for use on CNC machinery.

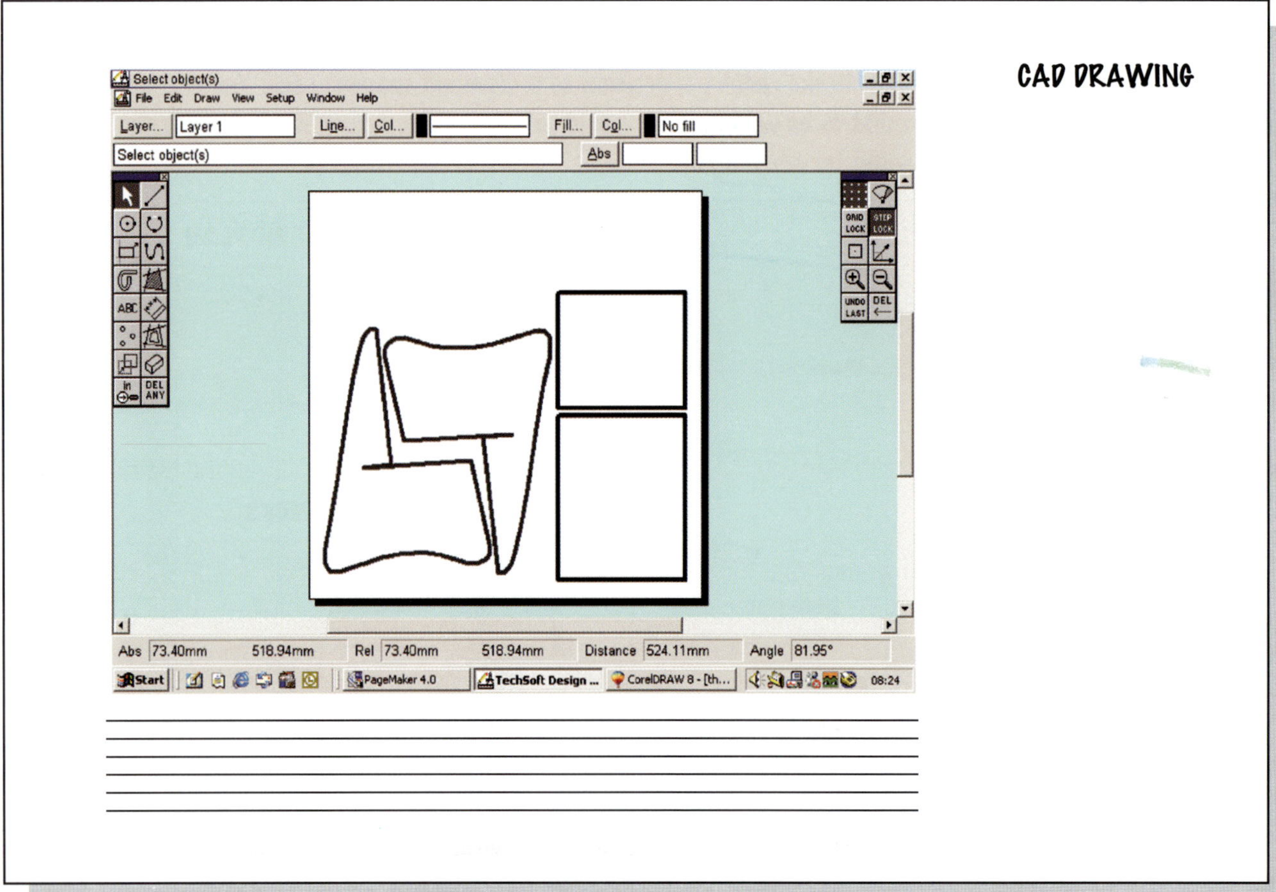

This design has been planned out so that the main structure of the chair can be cut out using a CNC router. Look at how the parts have been positioned to make the best use of the material. This is termed 'nesting'.

A screen print has been pasted onto the sheet and annotated so that the moderator can understand this stage. A printer or plotter might have been used to produce a working drawing.

This is one place in your design folder where it is worth spending some time presenting a really good drawing. This might be a CAD drawing or one using drawing instruments.

Design Proposals

What is required? It is unlikely that all of the information will be on a single sheet. Your design proposal will include production drawings, your plans and every piece of information needed for someone else to make your design from scratch.

Presentation Drawings

It is always important for your teacher and the moderator to understand what you are working towards. A really clear 3D drawing is one way in which this might be achieved. Modelling is the other method which might be used but it is often more time consuming.

Pro/DESKTOP

This is a piece of software which is available to all schools free of charge and can be made available to students. This software allows you to model your design in full 3D and to render it in any material. It is very time consuming to learn but if you have these skills now is the time to show off! This is exactly how commercial product designers operate.

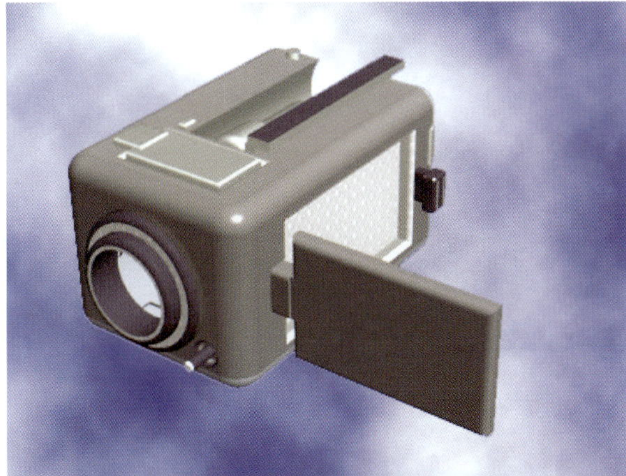

A fully rendered Pro/DESKTOP drawing.

Presentation drawings allow you to show different colour options and details such as upholstery. You could attach material samples, paint charts etc.

Evaluation should have taken place at every stage of the design process and the moderator will be looking for this evidence. It is usual to include a final evaluation report which summarises what you have done, how successful the prototype appears to be and what modifications need to take place before it goes into commercial production.

Evaluation Of Final Prototype

An evaluation should include a review of your final product using your judgement to assess its success. Asking other people's opinions is an important part of this process. A good place to start would be to answer the following questions:

- Do you find the product easy to use?
- Does it function in the way it was intended to?
- What do you think about the style of the product?
- Do you like or dislike any features? Explain why.
- Would you purchase this product and if so what would you expect to pay for such a product?
- What are the main advantages or disadvantages compared to similar products?

Specification

You should test your product against the original specification. Check your prototype against each of the criteria you originally listed. Was the design specification correct? Did you need to revise this as the work progressed? A simple chart might help.

SPECIFICATION CRITERIA	TEST OR QUESTION	RESULTS & EXPLANATIONS
Must fold flat.	How flat did it go?	The height was 77mm which was higher than expected. I forgot to allow for the size of the feet.

Get other people to write their comments on a similar chart.

Testing your product is an important part of the evaluation.

Testing

Companies undertake numerous tests before a product goes into full scale production. These can sometimes include testing prototypes to destruction.

You will need to ensure that your prototype does not get damaged before the moderator assesses it. You should have done this type of testing at a much earlier stage, if you think that it's necessary.

You should try to set up some field tests. They are tests which replicate real use as far as possible.

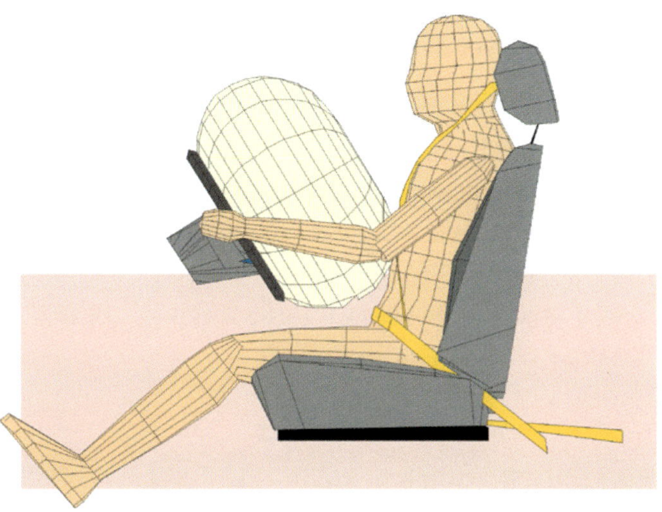

Get children to test out toys and play equipment. Ensure that they can come to no harm and always have an adult supervising the test.

Seek opinions from a broad range of people. Remember that products are often purchased for other users. Who would actually pay for the product?

If your prototype is easily transported consider showing it to relevant shops. Could they sell such a product? What would they expect to have to charge for such a product?

There is no such thing as the perfect design. All products can be improved. Despite all the time and effort you have put into designing and making your prototype there will be some scope for improvements.

Modifications Needed

The first thing to do is to respond to the tests and other people's comments. Issues such as colour are not usually very important and nothing other than a comment from you is required. If there are major problems with your design then you do need to respond in more detail.

Major problems do not mean that you will gain a poor grade. You could still get a high grade if your product is a complete failure. You will need to make some serious suggestions for improvements and might need to produce detailed drawings or models. You will need to ensure that you allow enough time for a full evaluation to take place, many students do not. Design work at this stage will be assessed under several headings so it really is valuable to your overall grade.

Modifications For Production

This is also an area you will need to address. The first thing to do is to arrange a meeting with a real expert (yes, your teacher!). They should be able to assist you with some of the answers. Make suggestions about the processes which might be used if your design was commercially produced. Comments such as 'I would use CAD/CAM' will gain you no credit. You will need to explain your industrial understanding.

Ask yourself the following questions:

- Would they use the same materials as I used in my prototype?
- Would the construction methods be the same?
- How would the surface finishes differ from my prototype?
- Can I make design changes which would reduce production costs?
- Is there scope for automating parts of the manufacturing process?
- Can I reduce the number of different components in my design?

A production manager would certainly be looking at these issues and would also be thinking about the production aids which would be needed.

Can you think of any aids which would help you if you needed to make ten or more prototypes exactly the same?

How could you cut the pieces without measuring them individually?

How could holes be drilled without marking them out individually?

Although you may only manufacture one final product from your design it is important that you are aware of the various possible methods of production and how yours could be produced commercially. You should explain this in your design folder.

'One-off' Production

This is when one product is made at one particular time.
It could be a prototype or a very intricate object.
'One-off' production usually takes a long time which very often results in the product being expensive.
A typical product could be a display for an exhibition stand.

Batch Production

A series of products (which are all the same) are made together in either small or large quantities.
Once made, another series of products may be produced using the same equipment and workforce.
A typical product could be a stool.

Mass Production

This involves the product going through various stages on a production line where the workers at a particular stage are responsible for a certain part of the product. It usually involves the product being produced for days or even weeks and in large numbers. This sort of production results in the product being relatively inexpensive but production could be halted if a problem occurs at any stage of the production line. A typical product could be a car.

Continuous Production

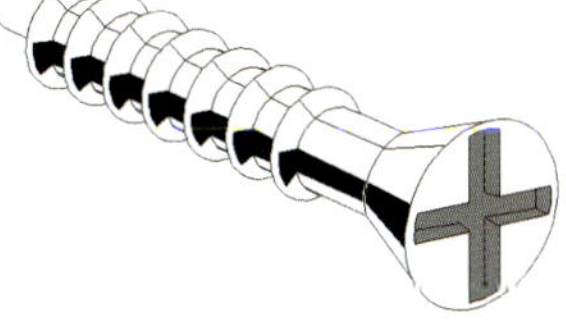

This is where the product is continually produced over a period of hours, days or even years. This sort of production very often results in the product being relatively inexpensive. A typical product could be wood screws.

'Just In Time' Production

This involves the arrival of component parts at exactly the time they are needed at the factory.
'Just in time' allows for less storage space thereby saving on costly warehousing.
However, if the supply of components is stopped, the production line stops which then becomes very costly.

Freehand Sketching

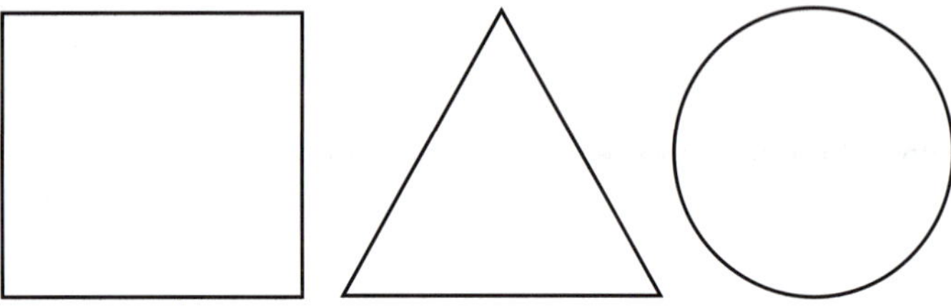
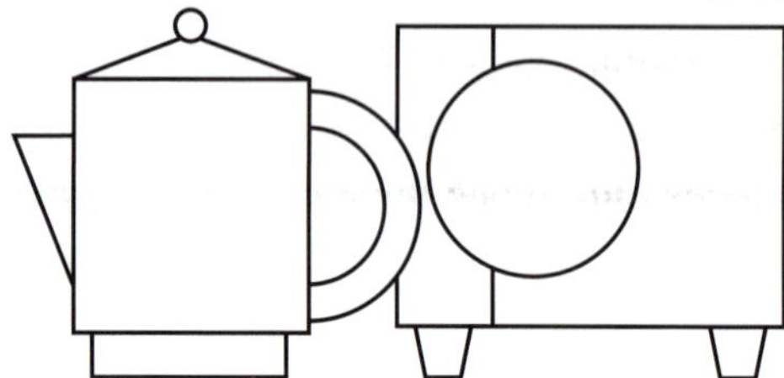

Practice drawing rectangles, triangles and circles. These are the basic elements of many manufactured products. If you combine them you can draw almost anything. Use a fineliner pen or ball point pen rather than a pencil (you can't rub the lines out so it will force you to work with more care).

Crating Out

This method is more time consuming but helps you to sketch objects in three dimensions (3D). If you can't draw straight lines then it would be a good idea to use a ruler when using this technique.

If you want to draw the following object ...

TIPS
Do not use this technique in your exam if you are asked for a freehand sketch.

1 First draw your crate, (a box). Your object will be drawn inside the crate.

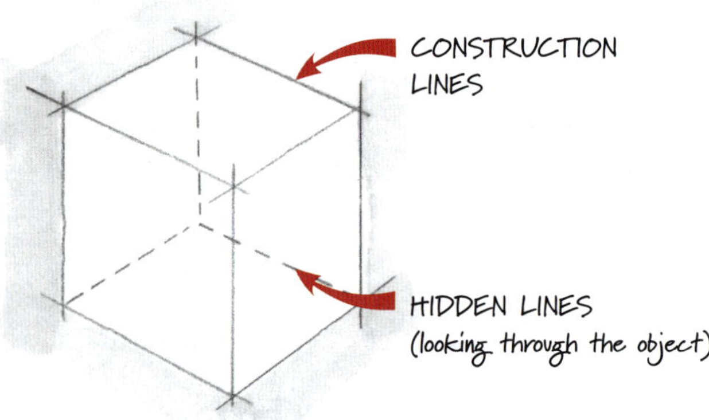

2 Draw one side of the object on one plane of the crate.

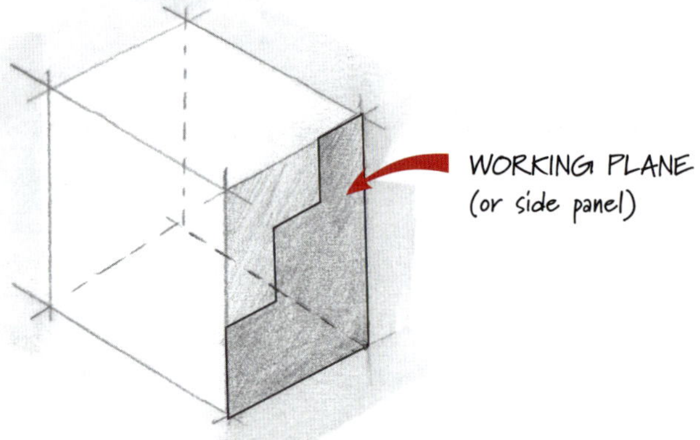

3 Reflect the side panel onto the opposite plane of the crate and draw the same shape.

TIPS
Leave the crate lines on – it shows the examiner how you have worked out your drawing.

4 Complete by drawing lines across from one plane to the other.

TIPS
Any line that connects two faces of the object, one of which can't be seen should be drawn as a thick line. Otherwise it is drawn as a thin line.

Rendering means applying colour and shade to an object to make it look realistic.

Tone

Tone is concerned with light and dark and can improve the illusion of a 3D object. Tone can be particularly effective in black and white, and also where there is a strong contrast between light and dark.

The most important thing to consider when applying tone to a drawing, is which direction the light is coming from.

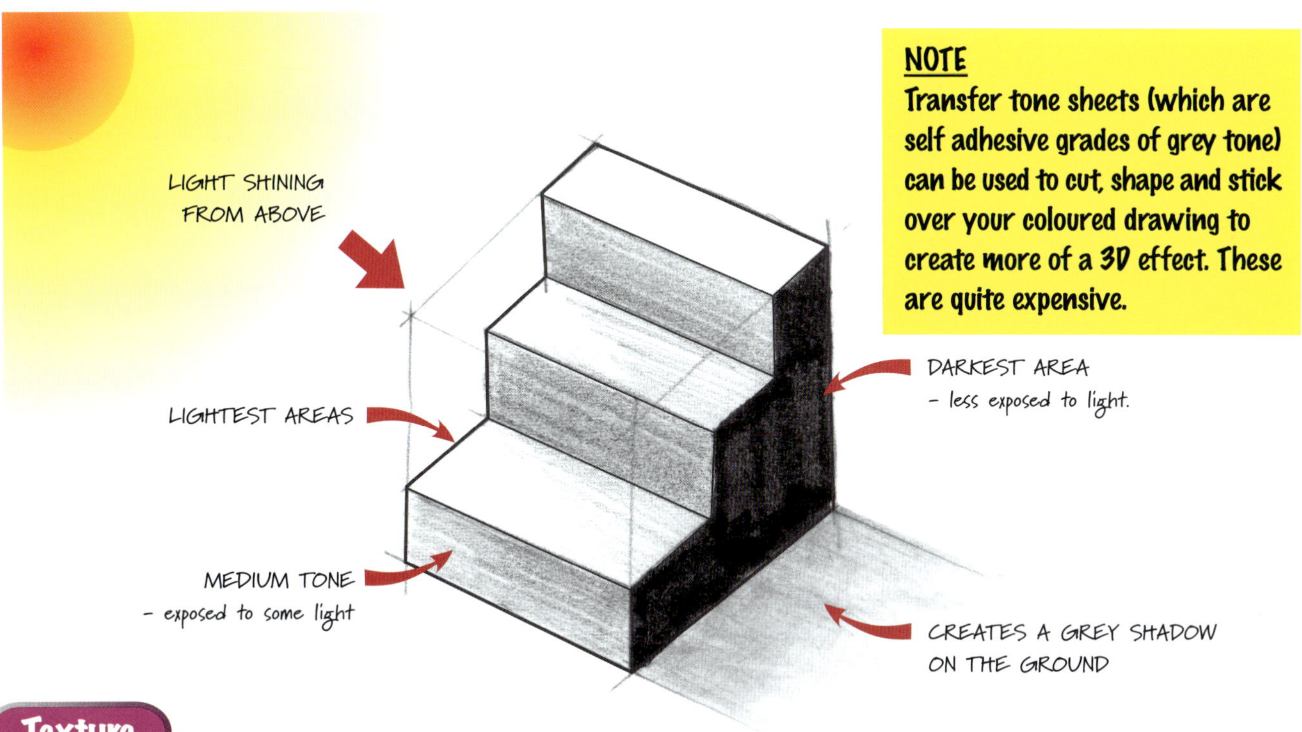

Texture

Texture creates the illusion of a surface effect. It is combined with tone to create a drawing that can resemble many different materials. Your choice of paper could also have an effect on the texture.

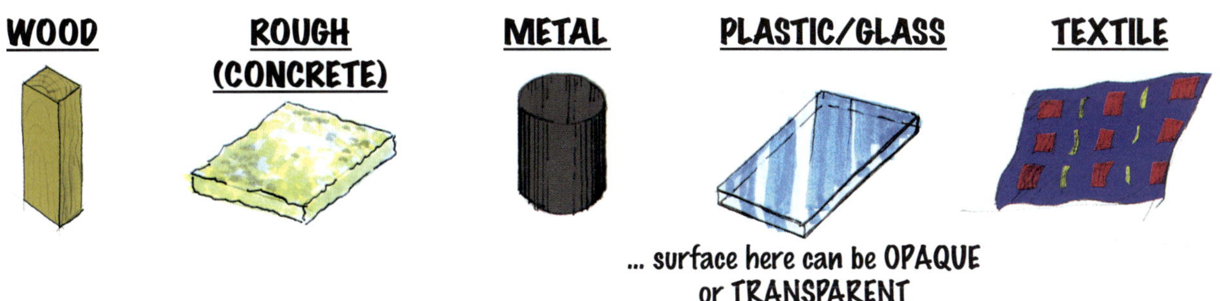

To achieve the above effects and to develop your own technique, try a combination of the following ...

- **MARKER PENS** - These are quick and effective to use. (Look at the illustrations throughout this book!)
- **PASTELS** - Are effective at creating tone - you must remember to 'fix' using a fixative as they can get messy. It may be necessary to fill the grain of the paper with talc before you start.
- **COLOURED PENCILS** - Inexpensive but can be time consuming. Can be used in conjunction with marker pens.
- **AIRBRUSHING** - Time consuming, very skilled and effective way of presenting final ideas.
- **PAINTS** - Again, time consuming and can be messy - watercolours are good as colourwash background.

Isometric projection is a drawing technique which looks fairly realistic and is commonly used to represent 3D objects. Its main advantage is that you can draw a 3D object to scale.

The following stages show how you can draw a simple cube in Isometric:

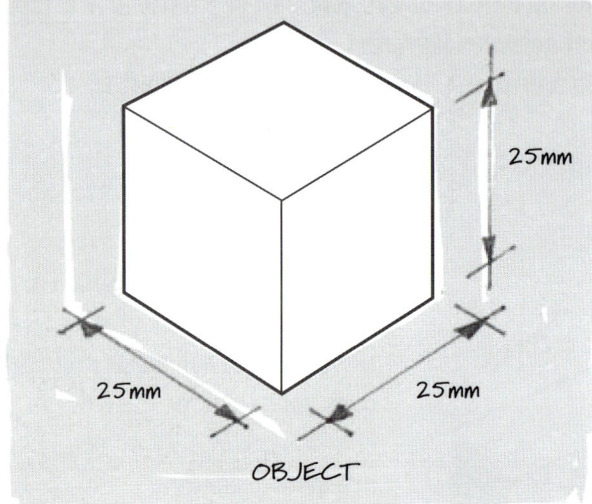

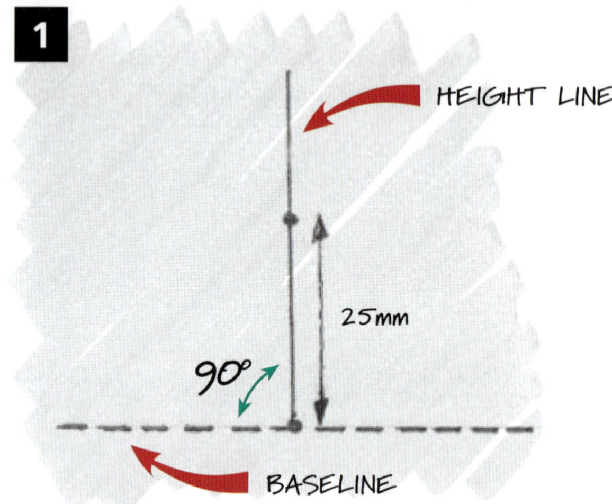

Draw baseline and height line at 90° - measure 25mm on height line.

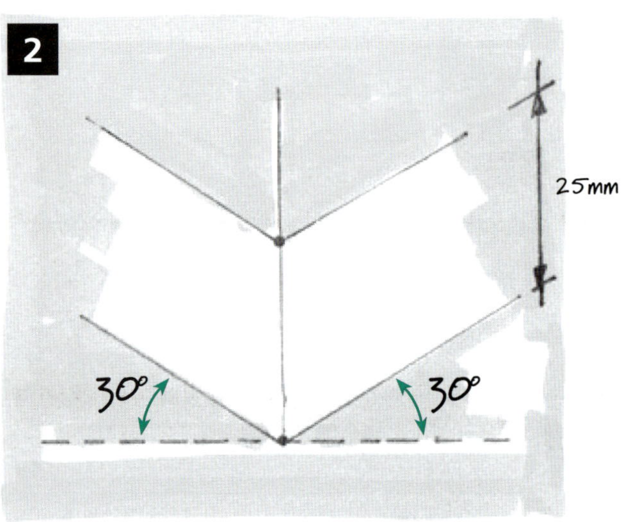

From each of these points draw parallel lines out at 30° to the baseline

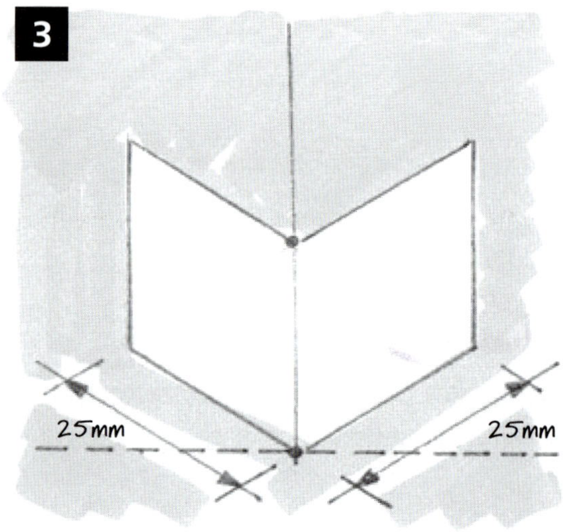

Measure 25mm on both sides of the base and draw two vertical lines - until they hit the top lines.

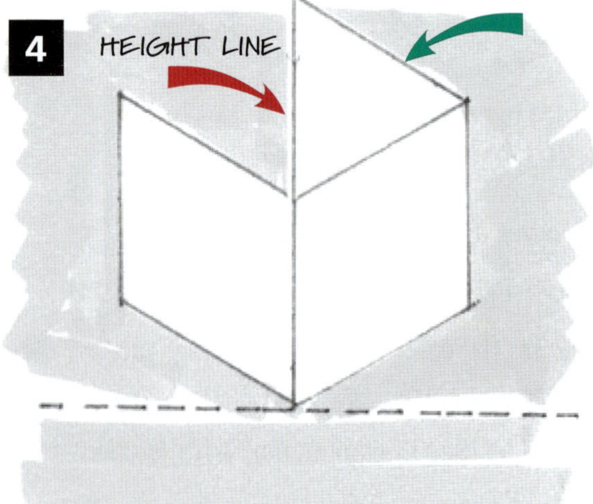

From the top right hand corner draw a line back to the height line which is parallel to the front left hand side.

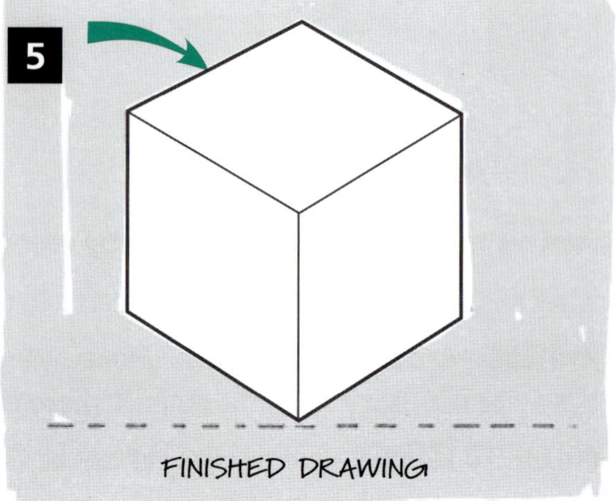

Draw in the last line in the same way and then rub out the construction lines you have used to help you.

Drawing Circles In Isometric

Circles in isometric appear as ellipses, and by far the easiest way of drawing them is to use an ellipse template. However it isn't too difficult to produce them freehand by following the instructions below ...

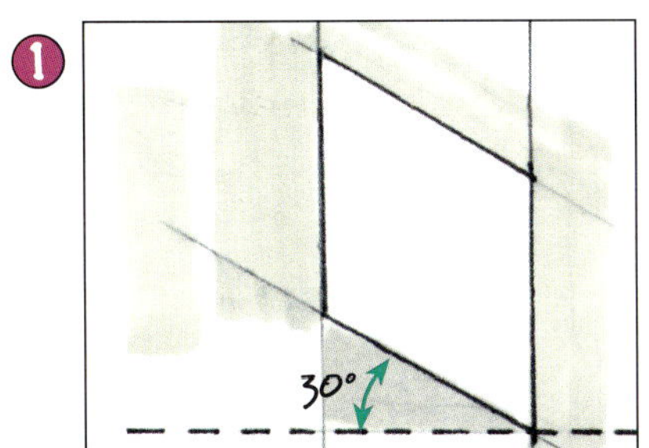

Draw a square plane in Isometric.

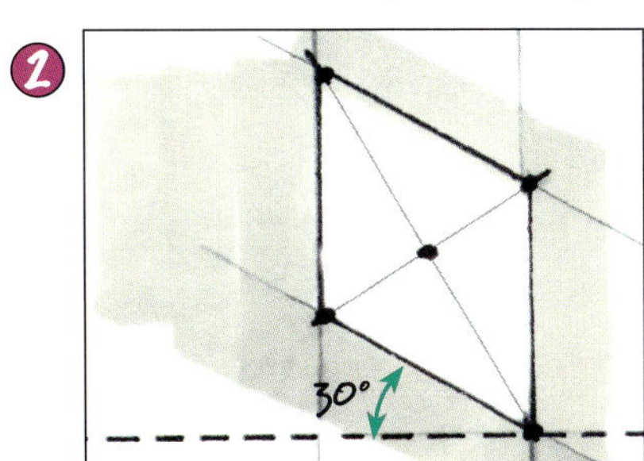

Draw two lines from corner to corner of the plane.

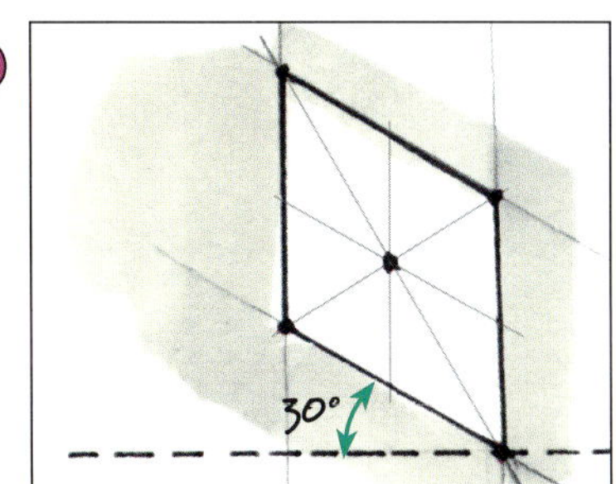

Draw two lines, one vertically through the centre of the plane and the other at 30° to the baseline through the centre of the plane.

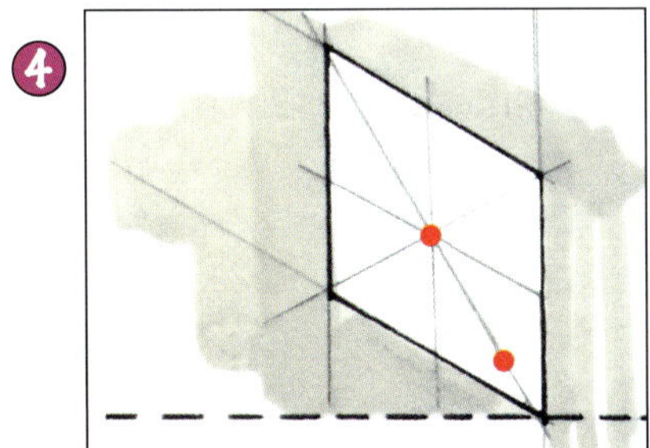

On the diagonal line plot a point $\frac{2}{3}$ from the centre of the plane.

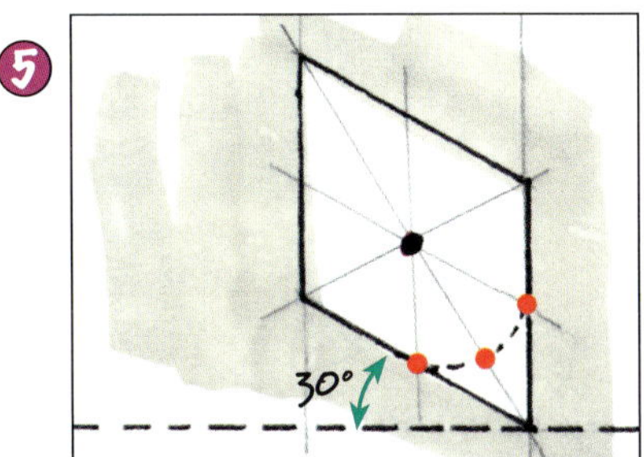

Draw an arc freehand through the 3 red points above.

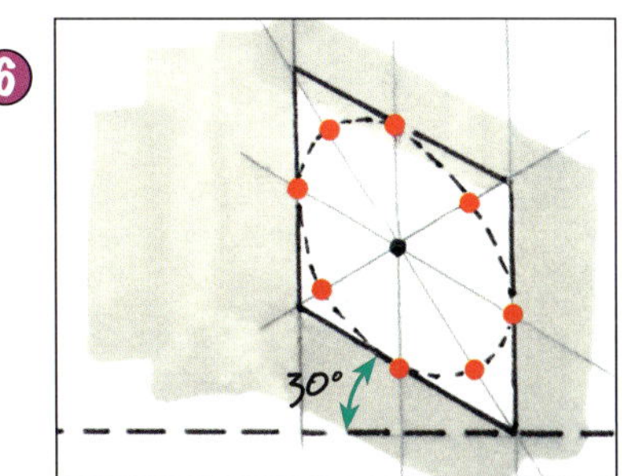

Repeat all around the grid until you have drawn the whole ellipse.

Exploded Drawings

Exploded drawings are used to show how an object fits together. Designers and Architects use this method, as it is quicker than drawing in perspective and helps them visualise what the object looks like, and how it functions.

Below is a picture of a pencil sharpener, drawn as an exploded Isometric.
The construction lines are left in to show how it has been drawn.

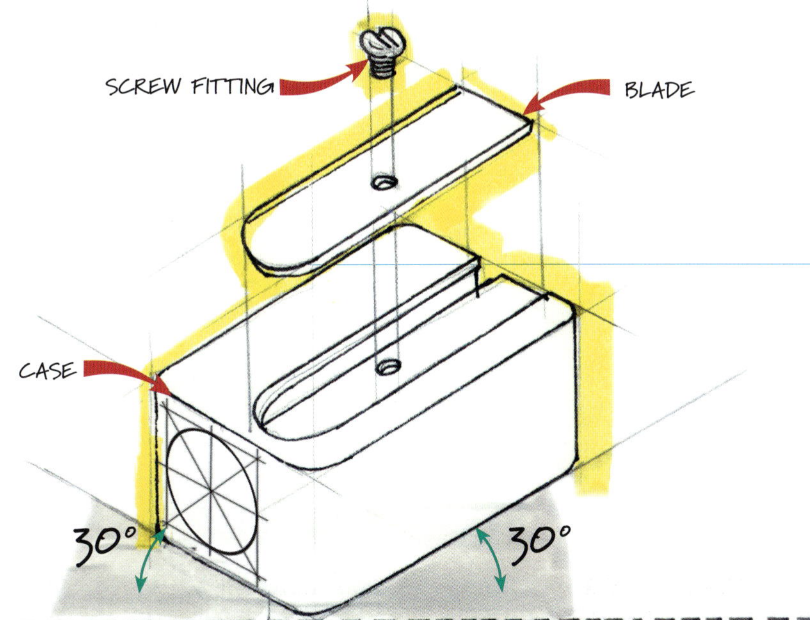

The designer will give a detailed drawing to a manufacturer or model-maker to make. The drawings give the necessary instructions for a prototype to be built. Each drawing produced should include the following:-

1. ACCURATE DIMENSIONS 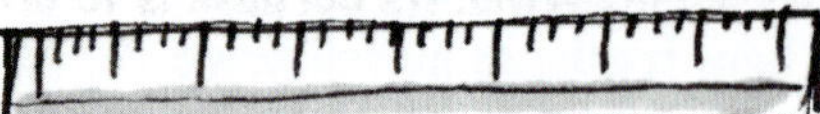

2. ASSEMBLY INSTRUCTIONS

3. SPECIFICATION LIST OF MATERIALS, COLOURS AND FINISHES

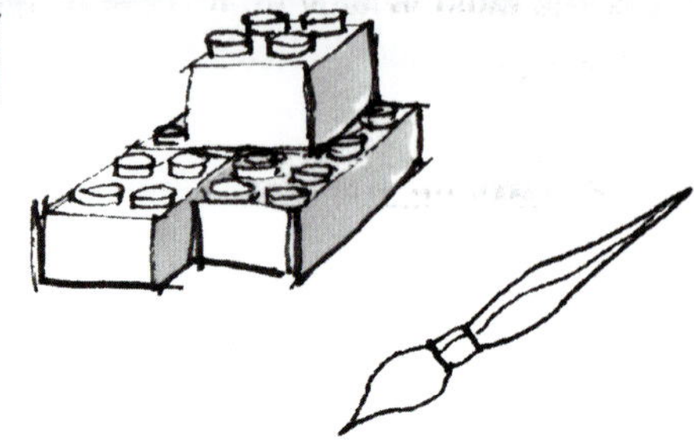

Standards In Working Drawings

The BRITISH STANDARDS INSTITUTION (BSI) has set standards in working drawings that are recognised throughout industry.

Here are some examples of the basic standards required for your GCSE coursework:-

1. Lines

- **CONTINUOUS THICK LINE** – For outlines or edges (could use H or 2H for these) where only one of the faces forming an edge can be seen

- **CONTINUOUS THIN LINE** – For projection or dimension lines (could use a 4H pencil for this.)

- **CHAIN THIN LINE** – For centre lines or lines of symmetry.

2. Dimensioning

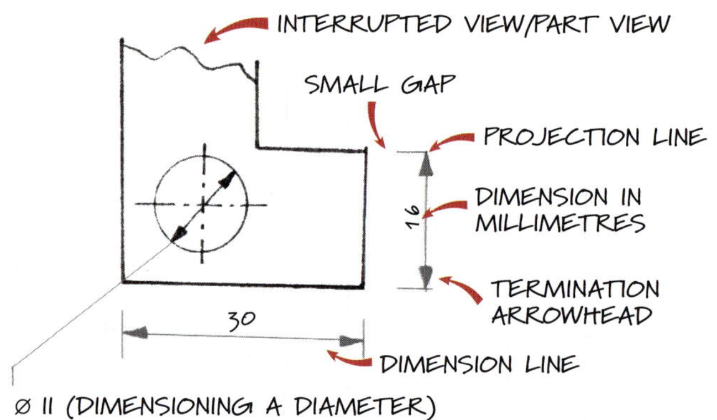

- Always use millimetres to dimension your drawing and write the number only ...
  ... this is the recognised measurement for industrial drawings.

- Numbers are always written above and in the middle of the dimension line ...
  ... with all vertical dimensions written to the left of the dimension line. (These are always read from the right hand side of the drawing.)

3. Third-Angle Orthographic Projection

This is the most common way of showing a working drawing. It is an accurate scale drawing of a product.

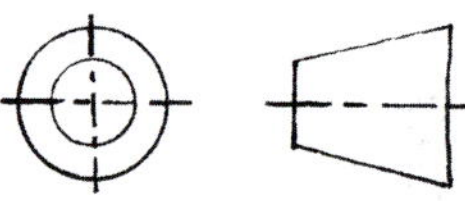

4. Scale

All working drawings are drawn to scale. The scale chosen must be included on the drawing.

Third Angle Orthographic Projection

This is the most widely used form of working drawing. Its purpose is to provide plan, front and side views of the object in question

THIRD-ANGLE VIEWS

- Imagine your product suspended in a glass box ...
  ... if you draw each view on each side of the box ...
  ... then open it up as shown above, this becomes your THIRD-ANGLE ORTHOGRAPHIC PROJECTION.

- Here is a stage-by-stage set of instructions on how to draw a THIRD-ANGLE ORTHOGRAPHIC PROJECTION.

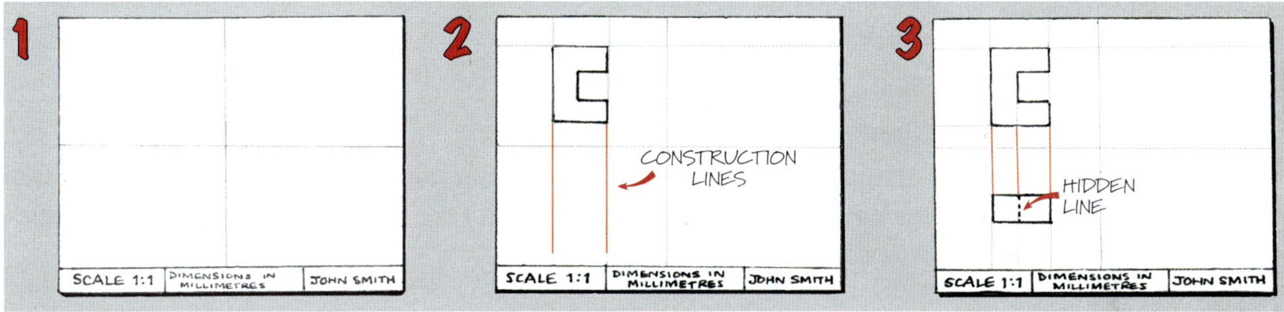

1
- Make sure you measure your page first - so all of the views fit on.
- Then allow a box along the bottom to put scale, dimensions and your name in.
- Divide your page into 4 using a 2H pencil.

2
- Draw the plan view first and leave in the construction lines, to help draw the next view.

3
- Draw the front view with the hidden detail drawn as a dotted line.

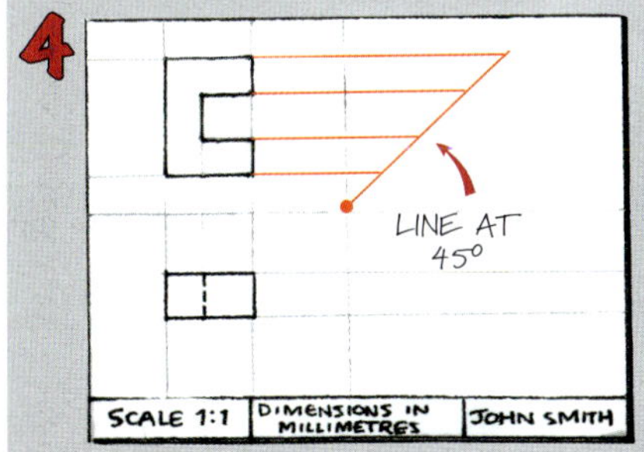

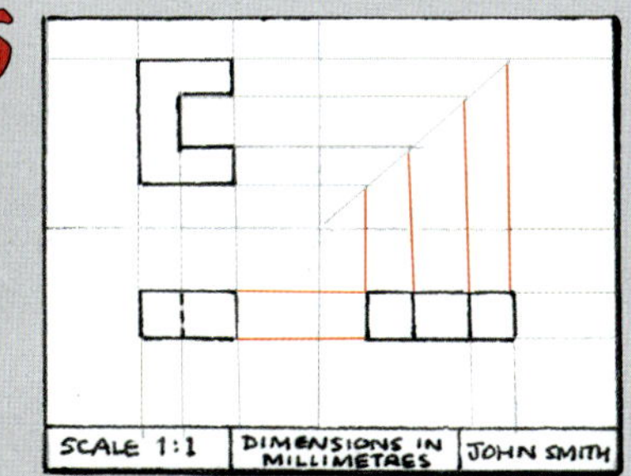

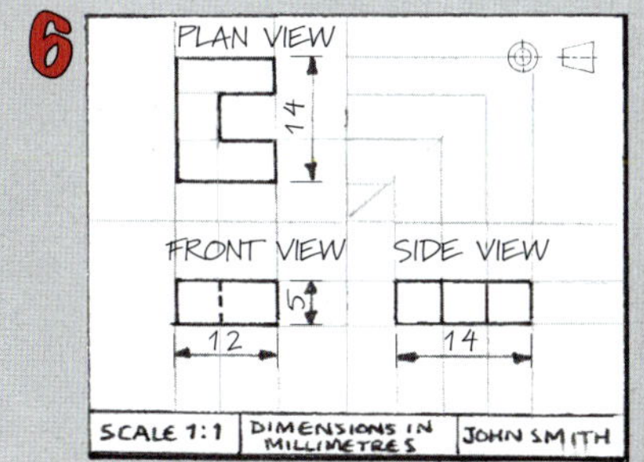

4
- Draw Construction lines into the top right box.
- Also draw a **45°** line from the centre of the page.
- Stop the construction lines where they hit the **45°** line.

5
- Draw lines down from these construction lines to join the horizontal construction lines from the front view, so forming the side view.

6

FINAL DRAWING

- LABEL VIEWS
- INCLUDE MAJOR DIMENSIONS

Using computers for your coursework could improve the quality and accuracy of your work. Hardware and software could be used in the following areas of your design work.

Digital Camera

Probably one of the most useful research tools. Allows you to photograph products as you analyse them. Can also be used as a scanner to capture images out of books. Digital cameras are also useful in providing evidence of practical work you have undertaken. They can be used to show:

- Models you have made.
- Prototypes made as part of an investigation of materials or processes.
- Testing you have carried out.

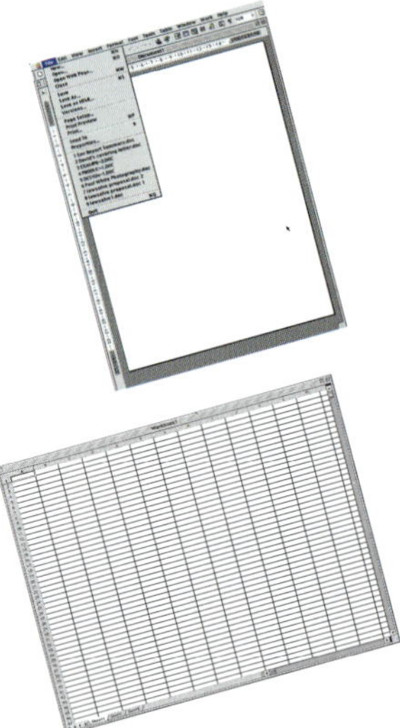

Word Processing Packages

Software such as Microsoft Word is especially useful for writing reports. As you can insert graphics and charts it is ideal for writing technical reports such as your analysis and evaluation work.

Spreadsheets

Software such as Microsoft Excel can be used to work out costings for your project. It is especially useful for creating charts to present research findings and similar data.

Desk Top Publishing

Software such as Microsoft Publisher can improve the presentation of your design work but beware of spending too much time on presentation, it's content which determines your grade.

Scanner

Apart from capturing images from books, catalogues and magazines, scanners can be used more creatively. Scan your rough sketches and trace them in a graphics package. Experiment with collage and other mixed media as a means of generating ideas.

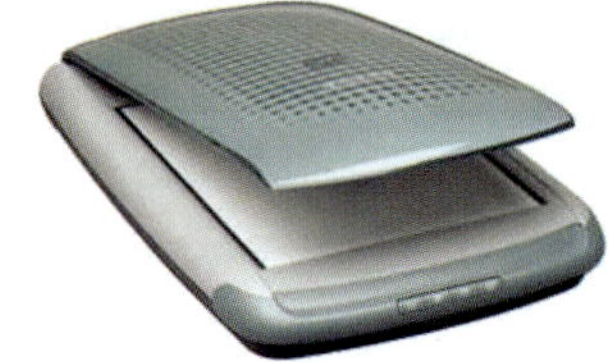

Graphics Packages

Software such as Corel Draw has lots of easy to use facilities. Can be used for producing presentation drawings and is especially useful when products require text or decorative images, such as children's toys.

Plotter/Cutter

Used for cutting self-adhesive vinyl sheet. This is especially useful where decorative details such as text or flat images are required on your product. One of the easiest forms of Computer Aided Manufacturing (CAM). As well as vinyl decoration, templates can be accurately cut as masks for stencilling, spraying or sandblasting details onto products. Can be used with a pen to create really professional technical drawings.

The Internet

Without doubt an excellent resource but as it's the world's biggest library it is easy to get lost. You will need to be very selective about what information you use in your project. Do not download masses of information and whatever you do, do not claim it as your own or you could be disqualified from the examination!

CD ROMS

Databases of information have advanced dramatically in recent years. Some contain animations of industrial processes, video clips and comparative data. The same warning as with the Internet, don't copy and paste into your project folder, be selective.

CAD Packages

Software such as 2D Design Tools, allows you to draw direct onto the computer and create the numerical code needed to drive a range of CNC machinery. Accurate drawings and a range of special features make this type of software ideal for this course.

3D Modelling Packages

Pro/DESKTOP and ArtCAM are both available free of charge for schools.

- Pro/DESKTOP is ideal if you need to model in full 3D.

- ArtCAM allows you to develop sophisticated relief designs suitable for making casting patterns or formers for vacuum forming.

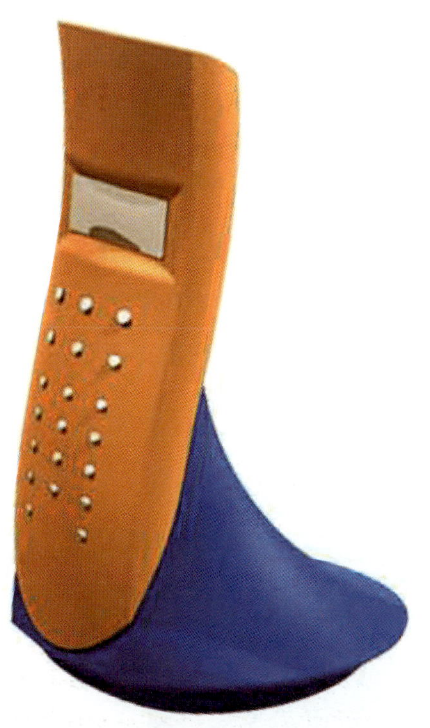

The ideal coursework project would use Computer Aided Manufacturing to produce components in quantity. There are many schools which do not have enough of these facilities to make this a reality but you should be aware of what is possible as it might feature in the written paper.

Computer Aided Manufacture

CAM relies on data known as machine code. It is numerical data which explains why the machinery used for CAM is often called CNC (Computer Numerical Control). Drawings are created using Computer Aided Design packages (CAD) therefore the term CAD/CAM is often used as a single process. Nowadays, the machine code is created by the software rather than inputted by a keyboard. This is known as Post Processing.

Two-axis Machines

This means that there are two stepper motors controlling the movements. One axis controls the sideways movement and one the front to back movement. Lathes, engraving machines, plotters and vinyl cutters work in this way. These machines are common in schools.

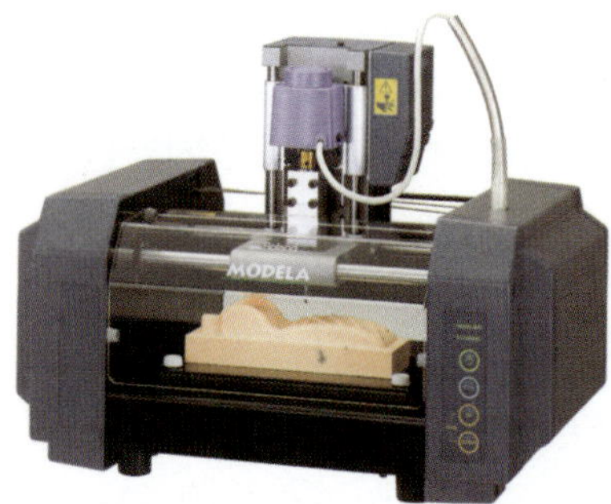

Three-axis Machines

A third axis, up and down, is added which means that more complex machining can take place. Routers and milling machines fall into this group. These machines are becoming much more common in schools and are used mainly for sheet timber and plastics.

Four-axis Machines

The fourth axis allows the work to be revolved at the same time as it is being machined and is very much like the addition of a lathe onto a milling machine. This means that full 3D can be achieved in one operation. These machines are very rare in schools but are common in industry.

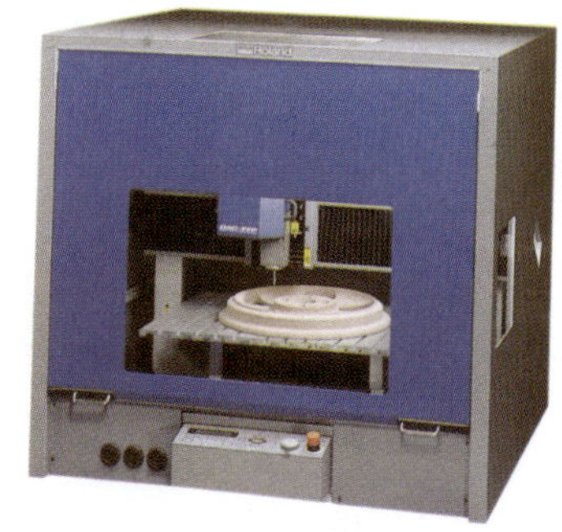

Rapid Prototyping

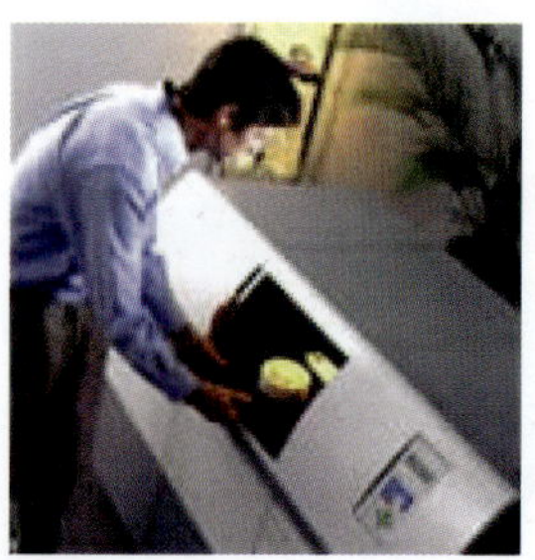

A way of creating full 3D objects direct from a CAD drawing. Builds up layers of wax to make prototypes. Used a great deal in industry but not yet found in schools. You can do something similar using layers of paper cut on a vinyl cutter but it is very time consuming.

Timber is the general name for wood materials. There are three main types of timber:

Hardwoods

These come from deciduous or broad-leafed trees. They are generally slow growing which tends to make them harder. However not all hardwoods are hard, Balsa for example is very light and soft.

Softwoods

These come from coniferous trees which have needles rather than leaves. Softwoods generally grow faster than hardwoods and are usually softer to work than most hardwoods.

Manufactured Boards

These are timber sheets which are made either by gluing wood layers or wood fibres together. Manufactured boards have been developed mainly for industrial production techniques as they can be made in very large sheets of consistent quality.

Natural Characteristics

There are five considerations when choosing timber for a specific purpose. These are:

Grain pattern - the growth ring marks visible on the surface.

Colour - different tree species differ greatly in colour.

Texture - different tree species have varied surface and cell textures.

Workability - some species of tree are much easier to work with than others.

Structural strength - different species vary from weak to very strong.

NAME AND DESCRIPTION		USES
BEECH A straight-grained hardwood with a fine texture. Light in colour. Very hard but easy to work with.		Furniture, toys, tool handles. Can be steam bent.
OAK A very strong wood which is light brown in colour. Open grained. Difficult to work with.		High class furniture, boats, beams used in buildings, veneers.
ASH Open grained wood which is easy to work with. Pale cream colour, often stained black.		Tool handles, sports equipment, furniture, ladders, veneers. Can be laminated.
MAHOGANY An easy to work wood which is reddish brown in colour.		Indoor furniture, shop fittings, bars, veneers.
TEAK A very durable oily wood which is golden brown in colour. Highly resistant to moisture		Outdoor furniture, boat-building, laboratory furniture and equipment.
JELUTONG A very soft wood with a close grain. Cream in colour		Model-making, used for casting patterns and carving.

NAME AND DESCRIPTION		USES
SCOTS PINE (RED DEAL) A straight-grained softwood but knotty. Light in colour. Fairly strong but easy to work with. Inexpensive. Cream/pale brown.		Readily available for DIY work. Mainly used for constructional work and simple joinery.
PARANA PINE Hard and straight-grained. Almost knot free. Fairly strong and durable. Expensive. Pale yellow in colour with red/brown streaks.		Better quality pine furniture and fittings such as doors and staircases.
WESTERN RED CEDAR Light in weight, knot free. Reddish brown in colour. Easy to work with but weak and expensive. Naturally oily.		Outdoor uses such as timber cladding of buildings, fencing etc.
YELLOW CEDAR A pale yellow-coloured softwood with a fine even texture. Light in weight but stiff and stable.		Furniture, amateur aeroplane building, boat-building, veneers.
SPRUCE (WHITEWOOD) Creamy-white softwood with small hard knots. Not very durable.		General indoor work, whitewood furniture used in bedrooms and kitchens.

NAME AND DESCRIPTION		USES
MEDIUM DENSITY FIBREBOARD (MDF) Smooth, even surface. Easily machined and painted or stained. Also available in water and fire-resistant forms.		Used mainly for furniture and interior panelling due to its machining qualities. Often veneered or painted.
PLYWOOD A very strong board which is constructed of layers of veneer or plies which are glued at 90 degrees to each other. Interior and exterior grades available.		Structural panelling in building construction. Furniture making. Some grades used for boat building and exterior work.
CHIPBOARD Made from chips of wood glued together. Usually veneered or covered in plastic laminate.		Kitchen and bedroom furniture when veneered or plastic laminated. Shelving and general DIY work.
BLOCKBOARD Similar to plywood but central layer made from strips of timber.		Used where heavier structures are needed. Common for shelving and worktops.
HARDBOARD A very inexpensive particle board which sometimes has a laminated plastic surface.		Furniture backs, covering curved structures. Door panels.

Metals are usually produced by mining ore from the Earth, then extracting the metal out of the rocks in a large scale industrial process. There are three main categories of metal although some will fit into more than one type:

Ferrous Metals

These are metals that consist mostly of iron and small quantities of other elements and metals. Ferrous metals are prone to rusting if exposed to moisture and can be picked up by a magnet. Both properties are due to the iron.

Non-ferrous Metals

These are metals that do not contain any iron at all. These metals therefore do not rust in the same way when exposed to moisture and are not attracted to a magnet. Typical examples are copper, aluminium, tin, and zinc.

Alloys

These are substances that contain two or more metals, and sometimes other elements, to improve their properties. The metals are carefully chosen and mixed to achieve specific properties which may include reducing the melting point. A typical example is brass.

Properties Of Metals

There are many properties which need to be considered when choosing metals:

Elasticity - the ability to regain its original shape after it has been deformed.
Ductility - the ability to be stretched without breaking.
Malleability - the ability to be easily pressed, spread and hammered into shapes.
Hardness - resistance to scratching, cutting and wear.
Work hardness - when the structure of the metal changes as a result of repeated hammering or strain.
Brittleness - will break easily without bending.
Toughness - resistance to breaking, bending or deforming.
Tensile strength - very strong when stretched.
Compressive strength - very strong under pressure.

NAME AND DESCRIPTION		USES
MILD STEEL Iron mixed with 0.15-0.3% carbon. A ductile and malleable metal which will rust very quickly if exposed to moisture.		Nuts, bolts, car bodies, furniture frames, gates, girders etc.
CAST IRON Re-melted pig iron with some small quantities of other metals. 93% iron with 4% carbon is typical. Very strong in compression but brittle.		Metalwork vices, brake discs and drums, car cylinder blocks, manhole and drain covers, machinery bases.
TOOL STEEL Also known as 'medium' or 'high carbon' steel. Up to 1.5% carbon content. Strong and very hard.		Hand tools such as chisels, screwdrivers, hammers, saws, garden tools, springs.
STAINLESS STEEL Very resistant to wear and corrosion. An alloy of iron with typically 18% chromium 8% nickel and 8% magnesium.		Kitchen sinks and general fittings in commercial kitchens. Cutlery, dishes, teapots, surgical instruments.
HIGH SPEED STEEL A metal containing a high content of tungsten, chromium and vanadium. Brittle but resistant to wear.		Drill bits, lathe tools, milling cutters etc. where high speeds and high temperatures are created.

NAME AND DESCRIPTION		USES
ALUMINIUM Light grey in colour although can be polished to a mirror-like appearance. Light in weight.		Cooking foil, saucepans, chocolate wrappers, window frames, toy cars, ladders.
COPPER A reddish-brown metal that is ductile and malleable. It is an excellent conductor of heat and electricity.		Plumbing and electrical components. Domed roofs are sometimes covered in copper which then turns green in colour.
LEAD A heavy metal with a blue-grey surface. It is very soft and malleable and has a high resistance to corrosion from moisture and acids.		Car battery cells, weather proofing for buildings, plumber's solder.
TIN Bright silver in appearance. It is ductile, resistant to corrosion and is malleable.		Most commonly used as a coating on food cans and similar packaging. Tinplate is steel with a tin coating.
ZINC A very weak metal which is extremely resistant to corrosion from moisture.		Used as a coating on steel buckets, screws and roofing sheets - galvanised steel. Die casting alloys.

NAME AND DESCRIPTION		USES
BRASS A hard, yellow metal that is a mixture of about 65% copper and 35% zinc. Often cast and machined, then chromium plated.		Decorative metal work such as door handles, candlesticks and boat fittings. Also used for plumbing accessories.
GUILDING METAL Another copper and zinc alloy but the amount of zinc is reduced to about 15%. This gives the metal a much darker colour than brass.		Architectural metalwork and jewellery. Often used in sculptures which need to be constructed from sheet metal.
PEWTER This is now a lead-free alloy which can be easily cast. It is mainly tin with a small amount of antimony and copper. Polishes to a bright mirror-like finish.		Drinking tankards, jewellery, picture frames and decorative gifts as a cheaper alternative to silver.
CASTING ALLOY (LM4) Mainly aluminium with 3% copper and 5% silicon. Looks like pure aluminium		Sand casting and die casting engine components, especially on motorcycles.
DURALUMIN Another aluminium alloy which is almost as strong as steel but 30% of the weight. 4% copper with 1% manganese and magnesium.		Aircraft bodies, some cars, door furniture.

Plastics have taken over as the most widely used materials in commercial production. There are so many different varieties with very different properties. Plastics can be created from two main sources:

Natural plastics - these include materials such as amber which is fossilised tree resin and latex which is a form of rubber.

Synthetic plastics - these are by far the most common and are chemically manufactured from carbon based materials such as crude oil, coal and natural gas.

Synthetic plastics are manufactured using a process known as POLYMERISATION. Polymerisation occurs when MONOMERS join together to form long chains of molecules called POLYMERS.

Plastics are manufactured using a process known as POLYMERISATION. Polymerisation occurs when MONOMERS join together to form long chains of molecules called POLYMERS.

Polymerisation is derived from the word POLY which means 'many' and MER which means 'part', so, for example... POLYSTYRENE is made up of single monomers of STYRENE, joined together to form a long chain.

<u>There are two different types of plastic:</u>

1. THERMOSETTING PLASTICS

Thermosetting plastics are heated and moulded into shape. If re-heated they cannot soften as the polymer chains are interlinked. Individual monomers are joined together to form a massive polymer.

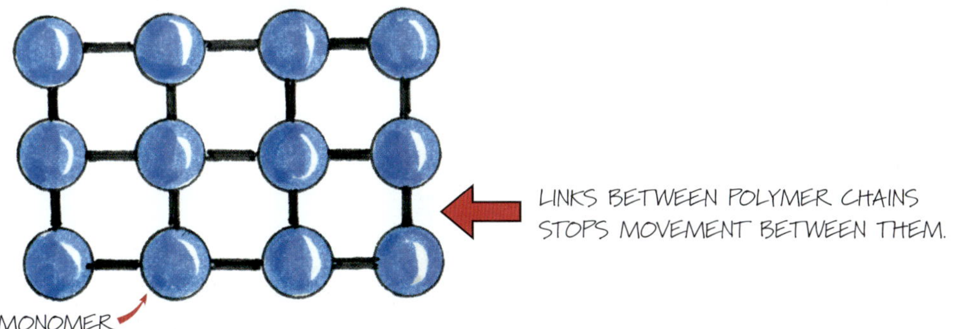

2. THERMOPLASTICS

Thermoplastics will soften when they are heated, and can be shaped when hot. The plastic will harden when it is cooled, but can be reshaped if heated up again.

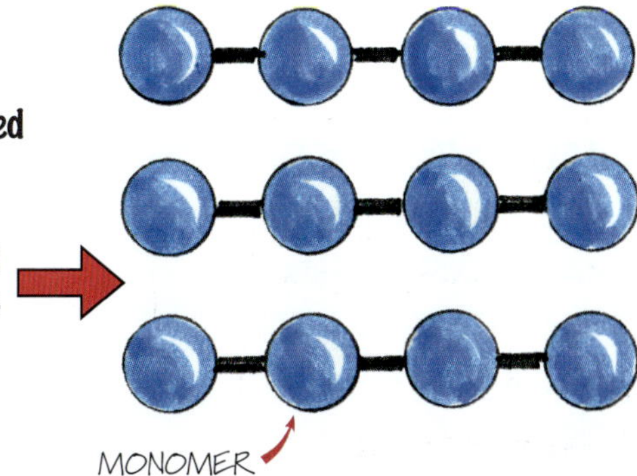

NAME AND DESCRIPTION		USES
POLYTHENE (HIGH DENSITY) HDPE Stiff, strong plastic. Softens at between 120-130°C.		Pipes, bowls, milk crates, buckets.
POLYTHENE (LOW DENSITY) LDPE Weaker and softer and more flexible than HDPE. Softens at 85°C.		Packaging, film, carrier bags, toys, 'squeezy' detergent bottles.
POLYPROPYLENE (PP) High impact strength, softens at 150°C - can be flexed many times without breaking.		Bottle crates, medical equipment, syringes, food containers, boxes, nets, storage.
HIGH IMPACT POLYSTYRENE (H.I.P.S) Light but strong plastic. Widely available in sheet. Softens at about 95°C.		Vacuum forming. Very common for school project work such as outer casings on electronic products, packaging etc.
NYLON Hard material - good resistance to wear and tear. Solid nylon has low friction qualities and a high melting point.		Curtain rail fittings, combs, hinges, bearings, clothes, gear wheels.
PVC, rigid (polyvinyl chloride) Stiff, hard wearing. Plasticiser can be added to create a softer more rubbery material.		Air and water pipes, chemical tanks, shoe soles, shrink and blister packaging. Floor and wall covering.
ACRYLIC (POLYMETHYL - METHACRYLATE) Trade name - Perspex. Glass-like transparency or opaque - can be coloured with pigments. Hard wearing, will not shatter.		Display signs, baths, roof lights, machine guards.

NAME AND DESCRIPTION		USES
MELAMINE FORMALDEHYDE (MELAMINE METHANAL MF) Heat resistant polymer.		Tableware, electrical installations, synthetic resin paints, decorative laminates, worktops.
EPOXY RESIN (EPOXIDE, ER) A resin and a hardener mixed to produce a cast.		Castings, printed circuit boards (PCB's), surface coating.
POLYESTER RESIN (PR) Polymerises at room temperature, a resin and hardener mixed together. Often reinforced with **GLASS FIBRE.**		Laminated to form GRP (Glass Reinforced Plastic) castings, encapsulations, car bodies, boats.
PHENOL FORMALDEHYDE (PHENOL METHANAL, PF) (BAKELITE) Hard, brittle plastic with dark colour, glossy finish. Resists heat.		Dark coloured electrical fittings and parts for domestic appliances, bottle tops, kettle/iron/saucepan handles.
UREA FORMALDEHYDE A colourless polymer - coloured with artificial pigments to produce a wide range of different colours.		Door Handles, cupboard handles, bottle tops, electrical switches, electrical fittings.

There is a growing group of new materials which do not fit comfortably into the normal categories as they perform differently to their close relatives. Here are just a few of the new and smart materials available.

SMART WIRE

A shape memory alloy (SMA) which is made in wire form is readily available to schools. By passing a small electric current through the wire it will shrink in length. When the current stops it will return to its original size. One application of this is the ability to operate lightweight mechanisms. Smart springs are also available.

LENTICULAR POLYPROPYLENE SHEET

An unusual characteristic of this sheet is that it appears much thicker than it is and objects placed on top appear to sink under the surface!

NICHROME WIRE

A resistance wire which heats up when electric current is passed through it. Can be used for cutting expanded polystyrene or used with thermocolour sheet.

THERMOCOLOUR SHEET

A self-adhesive sheet material which has been printed with liquid crystal 'ink'. Colour changes occur above 27 degrees. When used with nichrome wire, dramatic effects are possible on the 'screen'. Plenty of scope when designing children's toys and games, additions to jewellery, temperature indicators on products which heat up etc.

SMART COLOURS

A range of pigments which react to changes in temperature or glow in the dark. Simply mixed with acrylic paint they can make your designs really exciting.

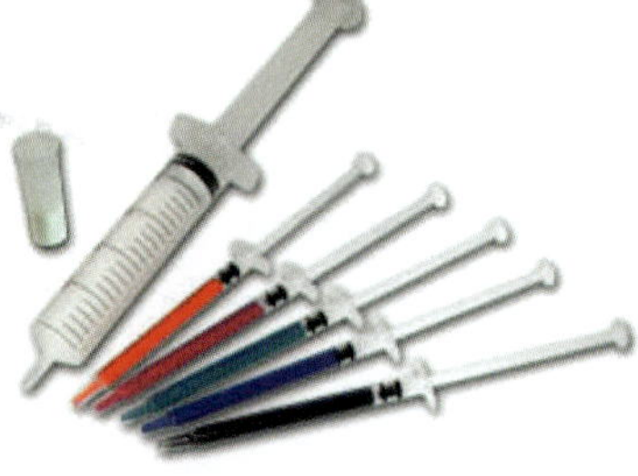

POLYMORPH

A tough polymer (plastic) which softens and becomes easy to mould at just 62 degrees. This means that it can be softened with hot water or a hairdryer and moulded into shape by hand. It hardens to a very stiff plastic. It can be used, for example, for tool handles.

SMART GREASE

A very sticky and viscous gel which can be used to control the movement of mechanisms. For example, on a rubber band-driven toy it can regulate the speed at which the potential energy is released.

Check out these materials on TEP's website: www.tep.org.uk

CONDUCTIVE POLYMERS (PLASTICS)

Imagine the design possibilities if you can use plastic products which can conduct electricity. These new materials are available to engineers who are starting to see the potential for their uses. Ask Jeeves about conductive plastics at: www.ask.com

There are many methods used for marking out materials prior to cutting or drilling. These might be categorised into the following:

TRY SQUARE

Used to mark lines exactly at 90° from the edge of the material. Having one accurate straight edge is a requirement before you can use this tool. Also used as a checking tool when assembling components which need to be square.

SCRIBER

A sharp tool for marking accurate lines on metals and plastics.

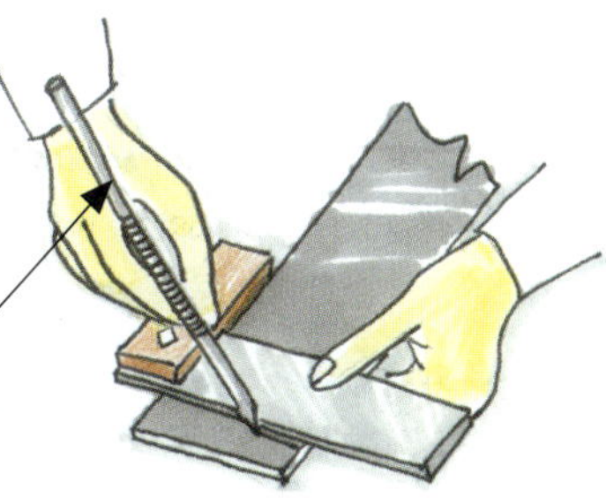

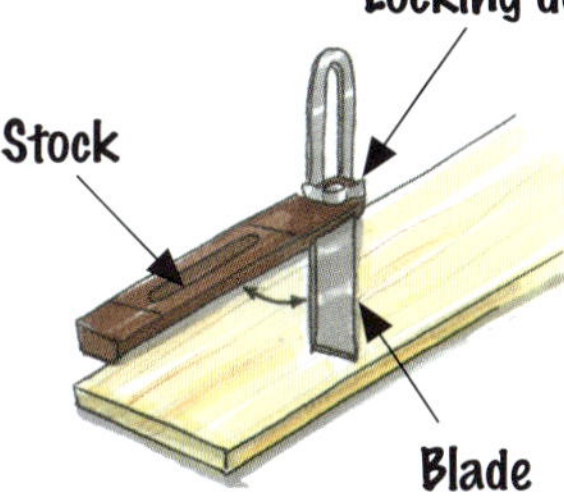

BEVELS

Available as fixed angles of 45° for example, or as an adjustable tool for marking any angle. Used in the same way as a try square.

DIVIDERS

Used to mark out circles or arcs. One point digs into the material whilst the other point scribes a line into the surface of the material. You need to mark the underside of the material if the surface will be seen.

CENTRE PUNCH

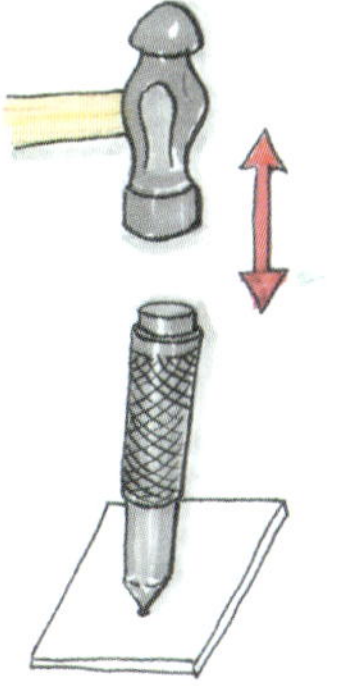

Used traditionally for marking the centre of holes for drilling into metal. The punch leaves a small indentation which prevents the drill bit from wandering across the surface. You can use this method on soft plastics and even on timber.

MARKING GAUGE

A simple tool for scribing lines parallel to a straight edge on timber. It can easily be drilled to take a pen or pencil so that it can be used to mark a range of materials with more easily seen lines.

ODD-LEG CALIPERS

These calipers are used to scribe lines parallel to a straight edge and are used for marking metals and plastics.

CARD TEMPLATES

Used for marking out curved shapes onto any material. Symmetrical shapes are best done by folding the template in half and cutting both sides together. Remember to put any templates you make into your design folder.

Being able to hold the material whilst working is very important both for efficiency and safety.

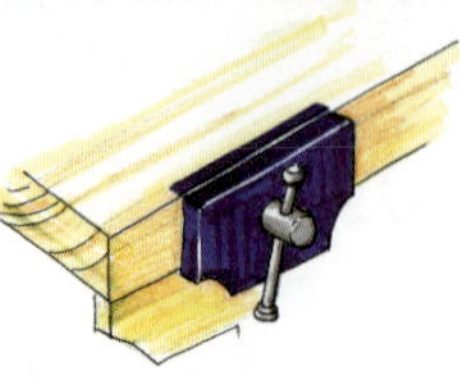

WOODWORKER'S VICE

With wooden jaws, this is used to hold timber and plastics to the workbench whilst they are being cut and shaped

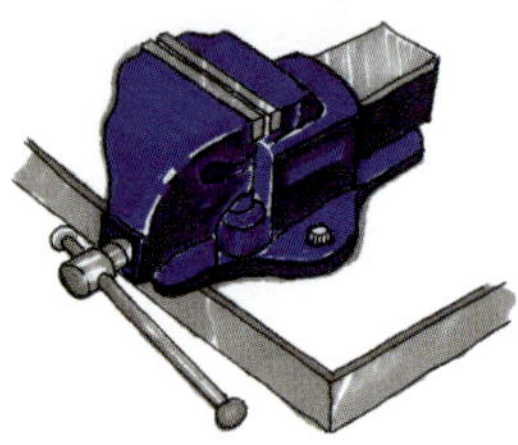

METALWORK OR ENGINEER'S VICE

A vice which is raised above the workbench and is available with hard steel jaws for heavy metalworking or fibre (soft) jaws for lightweight metal and especially plastics

G CRAMP

Used for holding material onto bench tops whilst working and for holding whilst gluing

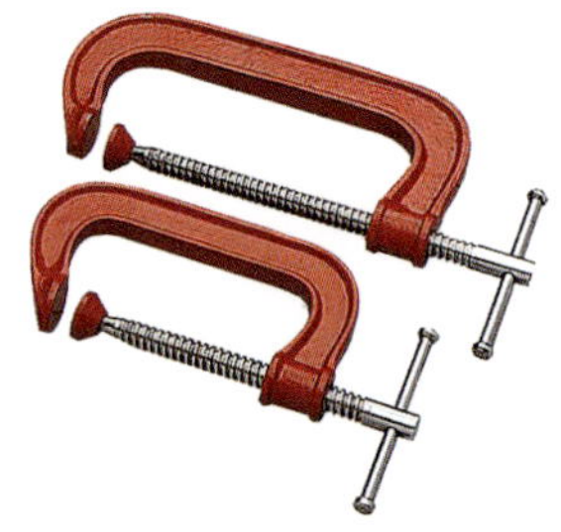

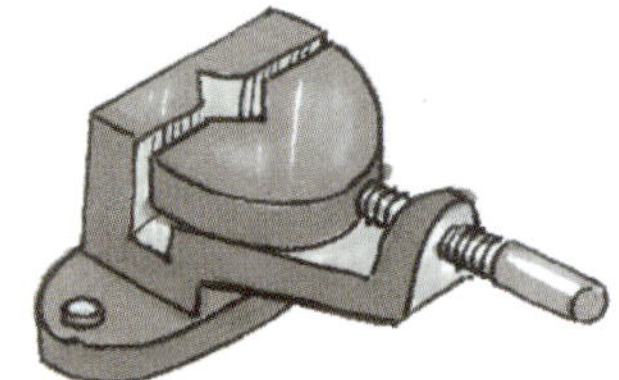

MACHINE VICE

Used for holding material whilst being drilled or milled.

HAND VICE

Used to hold smaller and irregular pieces of plastic and sheet metal that will not fit into a machine vice.

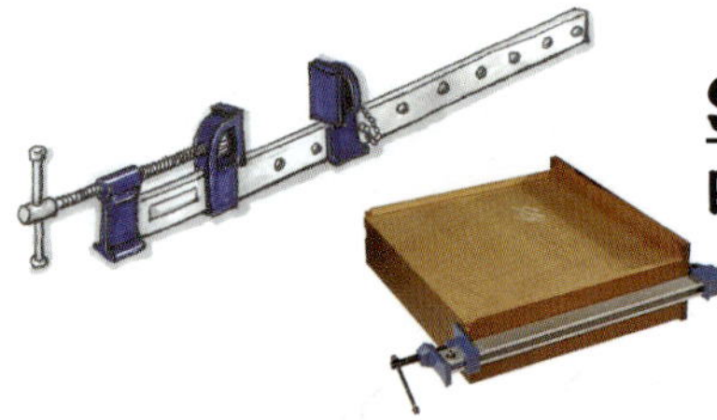

SASH CRAMP

Excellent for holding wooden joints together whilst gluing.

SPEED CLAMP

Similar to sash cramps but utilising a self-locking system which makes the positioning easier than a sash cramp.

CORNER CLAMP

Used for holding materials at right angles whilst joining together.

TOGGLE CLAMPS

Found as a fixture on vacuum forming machines but useful when creating jigs for volume production or used for clamping small pieces on a drilling machine.

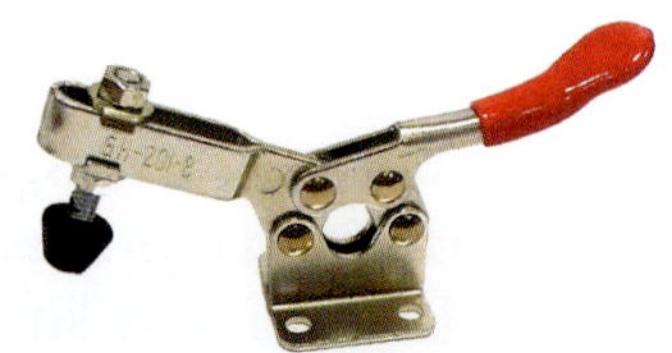

Jigs are holding devices which are used when manufacturing in quantity. They are often used for accurately drilling holes in components or for cutting material to size. You may need to make a jig or fixture to enable you to save time when making your coursework project or to ensure accuracy. You will gain additional marks for making your own jig or fixture but you must make it available to the moderator.

Jigs

Jigs are specially made for a component or are made adjustable for a range of similar operations.

Some jigs are commercially made for a variety of similar jobs.

Mitre box
Used for accurately cutting angles when making mitred joints, for instance for picture frames.

Sawing jig
An adjustable jig for accurately sawing at a variety of angles.

Fixtures

Similar to jigs but these holding devices are fixed to machines to aid quantity production.

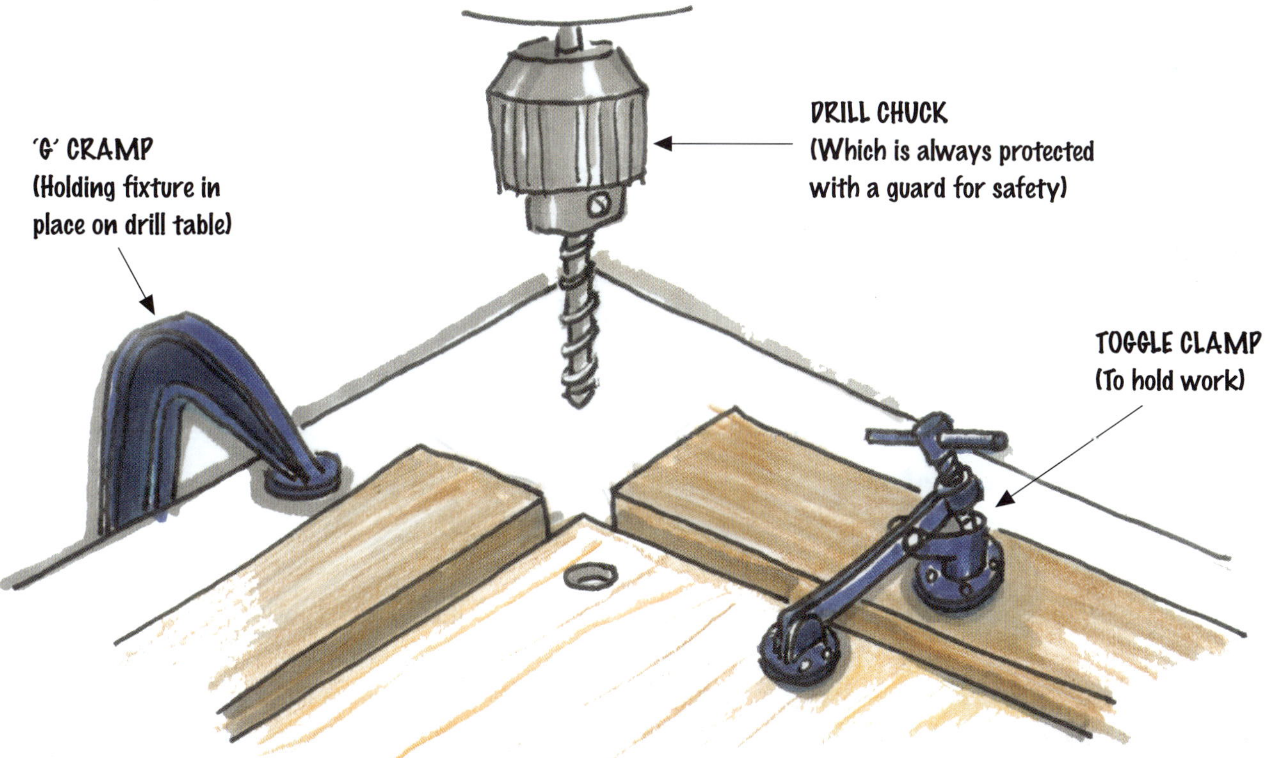

SIMPLE DRILLING JIG TO AID ACCURATE DRILLING IN EACH CORNER OF THE BOARD

Hand Saws

Sawing is one of the oldest methods of cutting materials. The principle is exactly the same regardless of what is being cut.

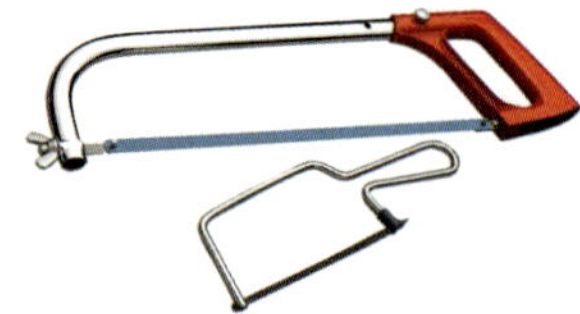

Teeth are shaped so that they remove a small amount of material on the forward stroke.

As a general guide, three teeth should be on the material at any time.

There are many different types of saw for different materials and tasks, some are powered. Hand powered saws work on forward and backward strokes.

Blades are sometimes held in tension within a frame. It is an easy process to change the blade when they become worn or damaged.

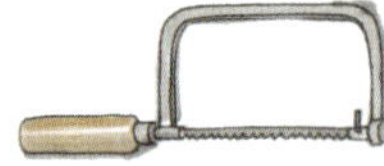

Wood cutting saws often have the handle fixed directly to the blade.

Power Saws

Powered saws work on several different movements:

Circular saws rotate the saw blade and the material is moved across the blade. These are used for cutting timber and plastics.

Bandsaws rotate a continuous strip of saw blade. Blades are available for cutting timber, plastics and thin sheet metals.

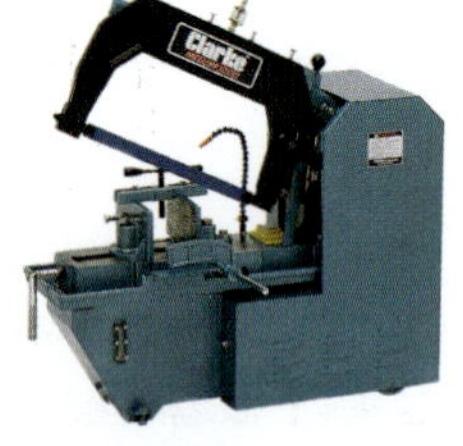

Powered hacksaws use a forward/backwards motion which copies the manual version and is driven by a crank slider mechanism.

Jigsaws move the blade up and down (reciprocating motion). The work is clamped to a bench and the blade is pushed through the material. Although blades are available for plastics and metals, jigsaws are used mainly for cutting sheet timber.

Scroll saws also use a reciprocating motion but the blade is held in tension and moves up and down through a table which can be angled. Blades are available for sheet timber, plastics and metals.

Chiselling is a process which can be used on timber and metals. Wood chisels are used on timber and cold chisels on metal. Chiselling involves using a wedge shaped cutting action.

Chiselling Wood

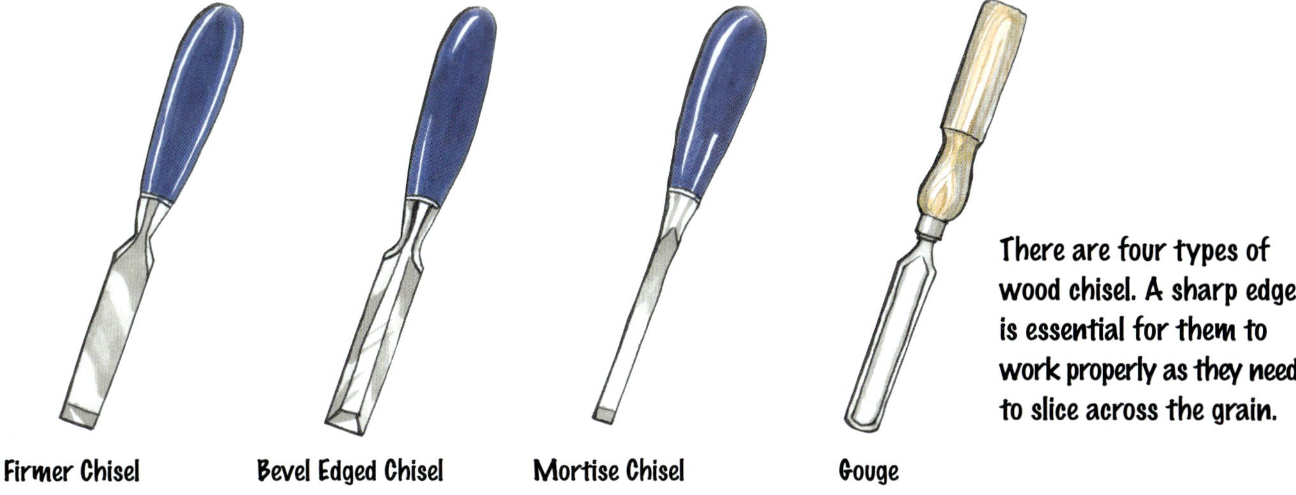

There are four types of wood chisel. A sharp edge is essential for them to work properly as they need to slice across the grain.

Basic Chiselling Actions

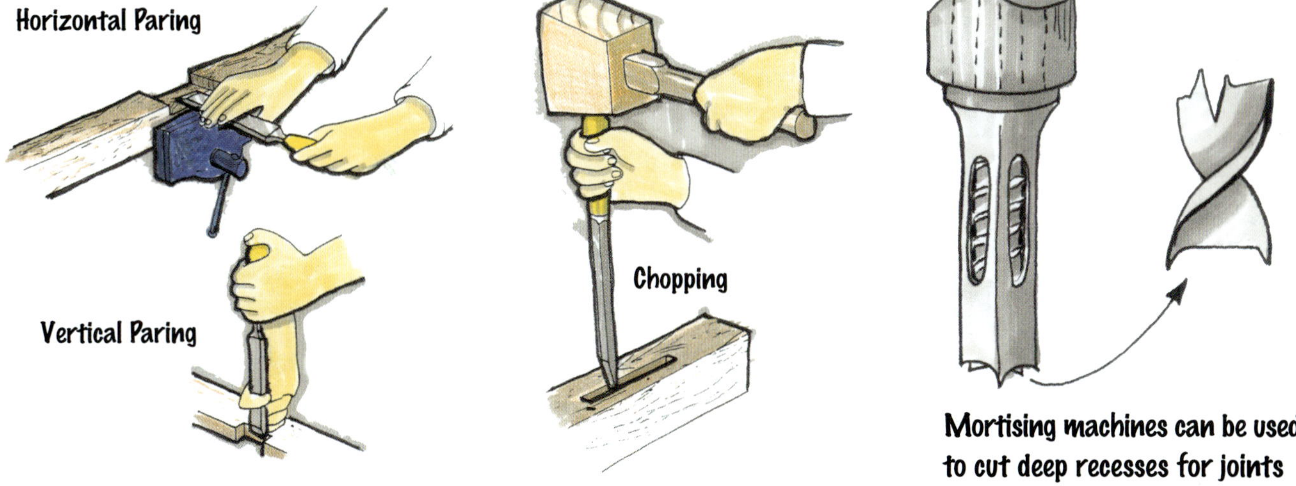

Mortising machines can be used to cut deep recesses for joints

Chiselling Metals

Cold chisels are made from steel which is hardened and tempered at the cutting edge. The other end of the chisel is soft to enable it to withstand hammer blows.

Hand Planing

Planing works on a wedge-shaped cutting action and is used to shave off thin layers of timber. Planing can be carried out on some plastics.

Smoothing plane

Block plane

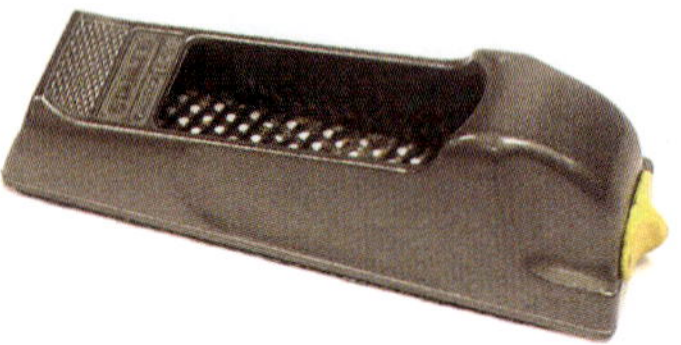

Surform

BASIC PLANING ACTION

There are some specially adapted planes which are designed for specific tasks

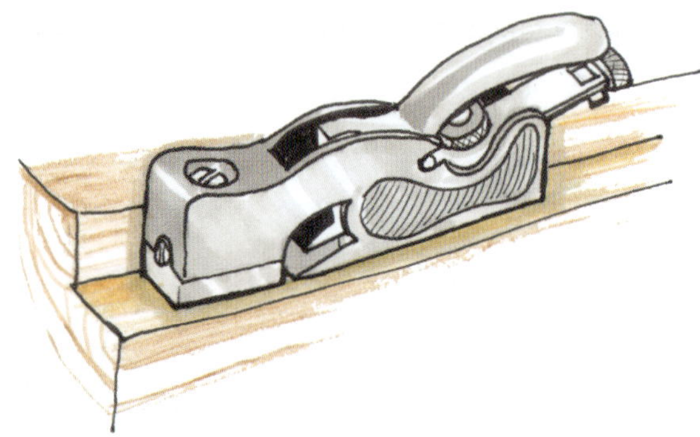

A shoulder plane used to clean up a rebate

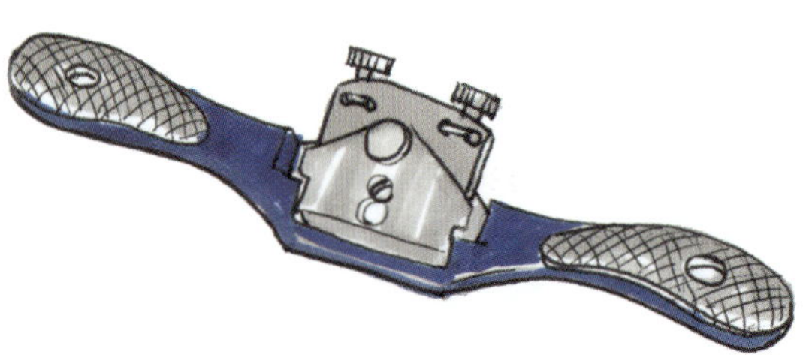

Spokeshave used for curved surfaces

Powered Planes

Many schools will have a machine which will plane timber. This is a common process in the timber industries and works by using a rotary cutter. There are also hand-held versions available

Rotary cutting action

Hand-held planer

Drilling By Hand And Machine

Drilling is the process of making holes by rotating a drill or boring bit. All resistant materials can be drilled, it is simply a matter of matching the correct drill bit to the material. Drill bits are usually made from carbon steel or high speed steel (HSS) although tungsten-tipped bits are used for drilling into brick walls, ceramics and glass.

All drills work on the same principle. The drill bit (or cutter) is rotated in a clockwise direction either by a hand-powered or electrically-powered device and is pressed onto the material surface. The drill bits are designed to cut and remove the waste material although the shapes vary enormously.

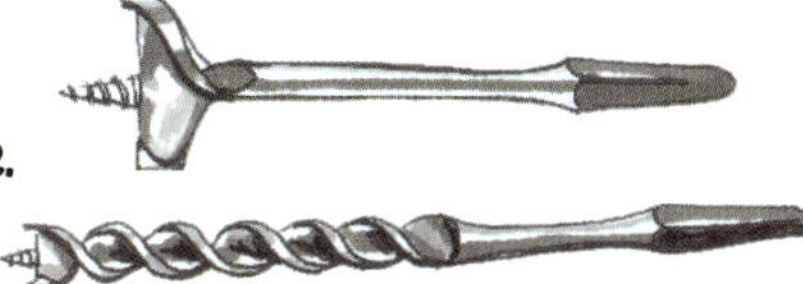

Centre bits and Jennings type auger bits are used with a carpenter's brace.

Forstner bits can be used on timber and some plastics to produce clean, flat bottomed holes.

Twist drills or jobbers drills, are used for drilling smaller diameter holes in timber, metals and plastics. They are unsuitable for larger diameters in wood as they leave a ragged edge to the hole. 

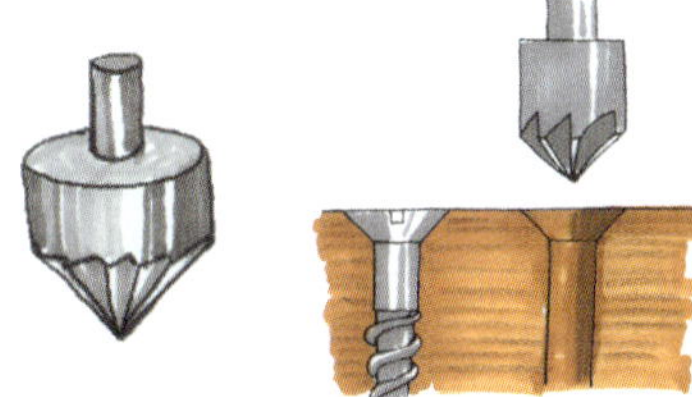

Countersink bits are used to allow screw heads to finish flush with the surface of the material.

Hole saws are used for cutting large diameters in thin materials. 

Power Drills

Portable power drills are commonplace and are available in mains or battery options. They are easy to use but do need the material to be firmly held in place.

Pedestal Drills

Pedestal drills (also known as pillar drills and drill presses) can be bench or floor mounted. They provide the safest and easiest method of drilling materials which can be lifted onto the drilling table.

Milling and routing use the same principle of a revolving multi-toothed cutter being moved over the material which is being shaped. When using this technique with metals and plastics it would be known as milling. On timber it would be called routing.

Routing

Shapes can be cut by manually using a powered router. This can be used to follow a template, used with a guide to cut slots or used to shape the edge of a timber board.

A hand-held router with guide attached for cutting slots parallel to the edge of a board

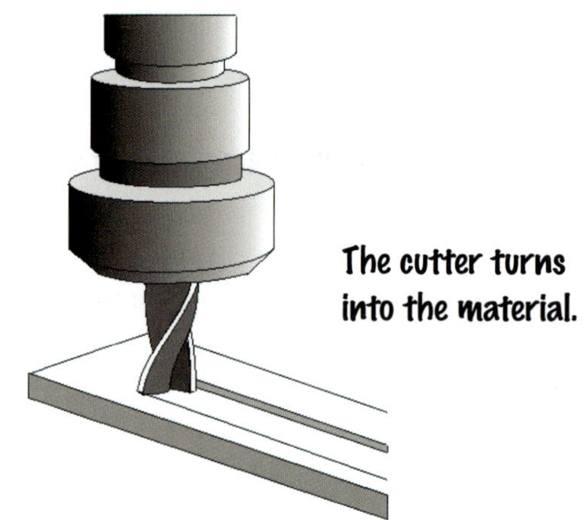

The cutter turns into the material.

Milling

Milling machines involve clamping the material onto the machine bed.

The cutter can be raised or lowered. This is referred to as the z axis.

The machine bed can be moved left and right. This is known as the x axis.

The machine bed can also move front to back. This is known as the y axis.

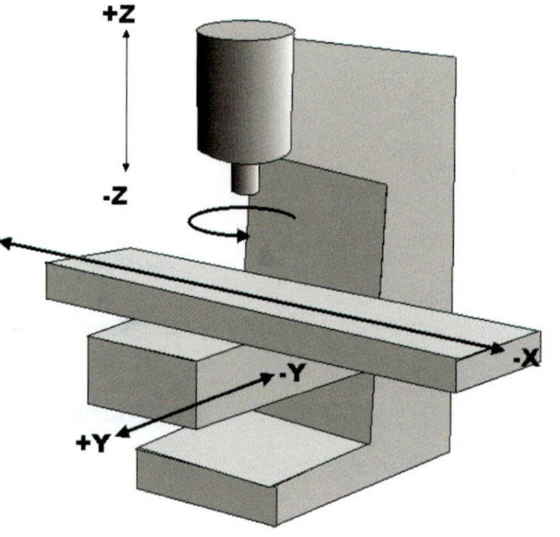

CNC Milling

Traditional milling machines can be controlled by moving each axis manually. By moving each axis with a stepper motor very accurate movements can be controlled using Computer Numerical Control (CNC). This is one of the most common forms of Computer Aided Manufacture (CAM).

CNC routers are very common in the furniture industry and work on the same principle.

As the name suggests, turning involves rotating the work against a blade. Wood, metals and some plastics can be turned although the machinery varies. Lathes are amongst the earliest machine tools, dating back centuries.

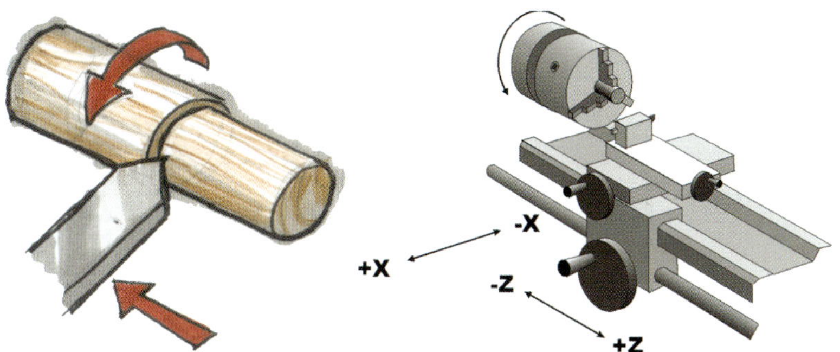

Centre Lathe

Turning metals and plastics on a centre lathe involves holding the work (usually in a chuck) and rotating the work towards the cutter.

The cutter can be moved left and right and forwards and backwards.

The tailstock can be used to support long pieces of material or fitted with a drill chuck for drilling holes into the end of the material.

Wood-turning Lathe

Wood-turning lathes are different to centre lathes as the tool is rested on a support and is guided by hand. Three different types of tool are used. These are chisels, gouges and scrapers. The work can be held between centres or screwed onto a faceplate.

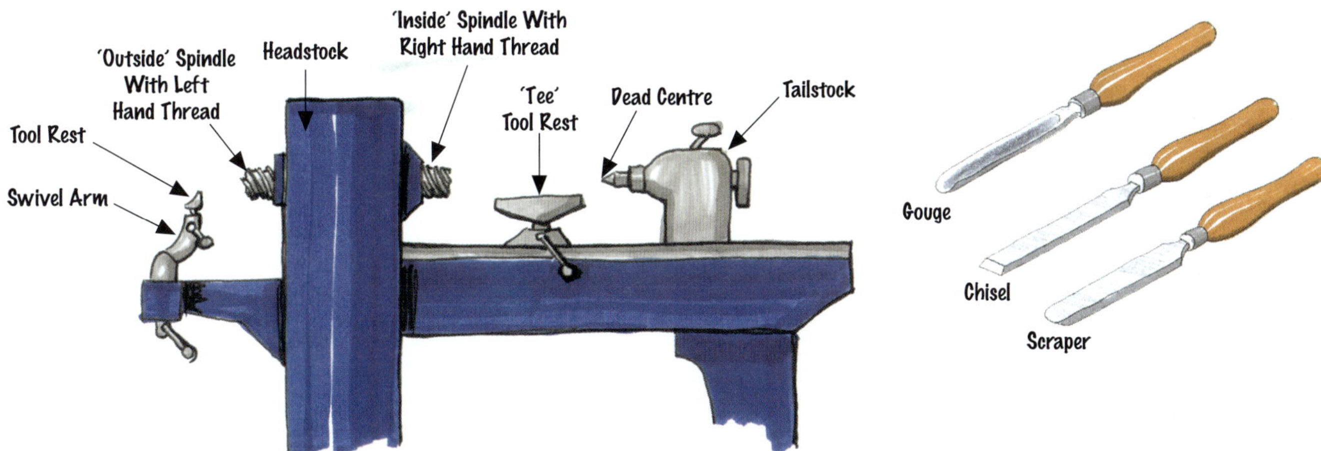

CNC Turning

The movements of both the work and the cutting tools can be controlled on centre lathes using stepper motors. This allows the lathe to be numerically controlled. CNC lathes are particularly useful for turning quantities of identical pieces.

Abrading can be achieved using a wide range of tools which cut away very small particles of material. These include abrasive papers and files.

Abrasive Papers/Cloth

The small chips of abrasive material are glued onto a paper or cloth backing sheet.

The abrasive material might be garnet, glass, silicon carbide or emery.

Each sheet is numbered. The smaller the number the coarser the sheet.

Emery cloth is often torn into strips and used in a two-handed manner. It is designed for use on metals although it is sometimes useful for finishing hard plastics.

Silicon carbide paper is generally a much finer abrasive paper and can be used either dry or with water. It is often called 'wet & dry paper' and is used for plastics and cutting back paint surfaces. The water helps to lubricate the cutting action and remove the waste material.

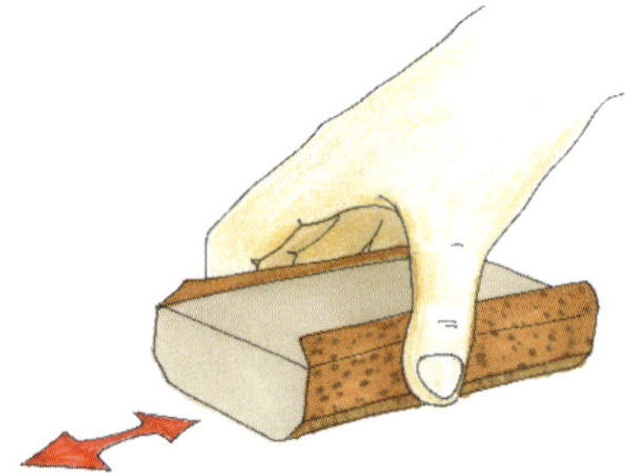

Abrasive paper is usually held around a cork block. Glass and garnet paper is used mainly for timber but is sometimes used with hard plastics.

Files

Essentially used to smooth and shape the surface of metals and hard plastics by pressing and dragging the hundreds of small teeth on the file across the material. There is also a type of file especially designed for timber called a rasp which has coarser teeth. They are made from high carbon steel and should be treated with care because they are brittle and can snap if dropped or abused.

Files come in lots of different shapes.

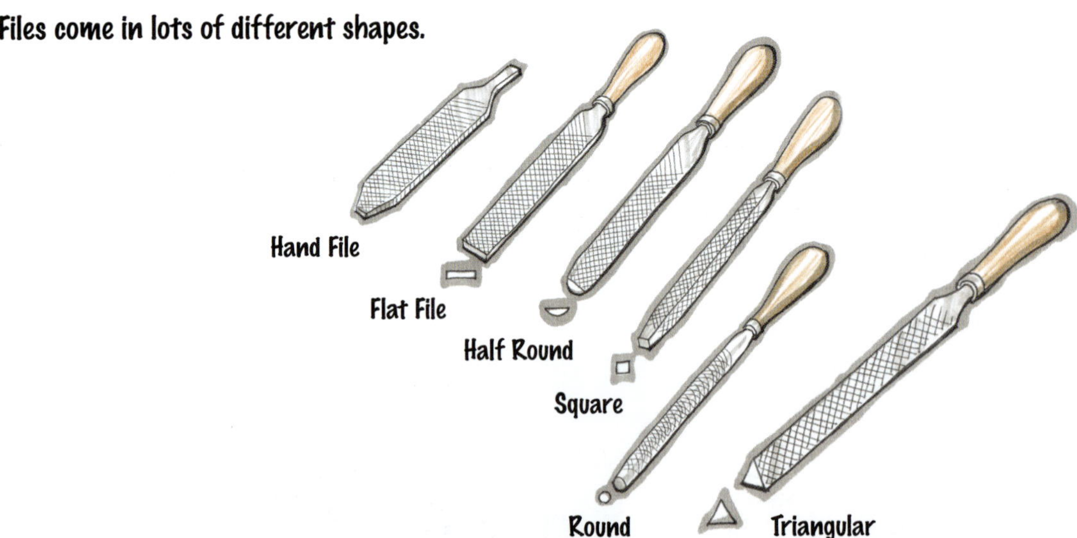

Sanding Machines

There are many varieties of sanding machines, all are designed to take off the material as quickly and easily as possible. In general, sanders can only be used for timber and hard plastics. Some machines are designed for metals and are called linishers. All powered sanding machines create large amounts of dust which needs to be safely extracted. The abrasive material used on sanding machines is often aluminium oxide glued onto a fabric backing.

Fixed sanders work on one of two principles:

1. Rotary Or Disk Sanding

An abrasive paper disk is fastened to a faceplate on the end of an electric motor.

Only the downside of the disk can be used.

The outer edge is spinning faster than the middle so material is not removed evenly.

2. Belt Sanders

Can be mounted horizontally or vertically.

A revolving belt of abrasive material is powered by an electric motor.

The belt needs to be supported along its working length by a hard metal surface.

Material is removed evenly, because all parts of the belt are moving at the same speed.

Hand-held Sanders

A wide variety of powered sanders are now available. Because they are both powerful and portable they do present additional safety issues. Always ensure that the material being sanded is firmly held in place and that any dust created is not hazardous to either you or anyone else.

Orbital Sander

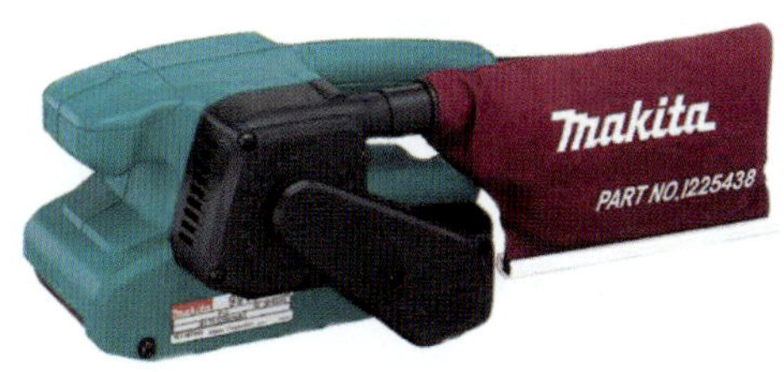

Belt Sander

Hammers are designed for a variety of jobs apart from knocking in nails

Claw Hammer

A heavy hammer which can drive large nails through timber. The claw is used to remove bent nails.

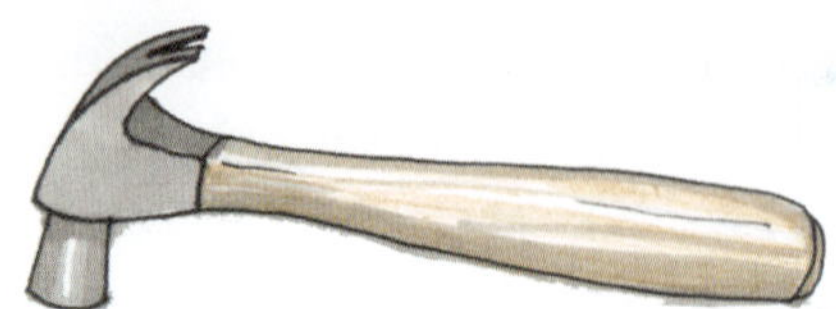

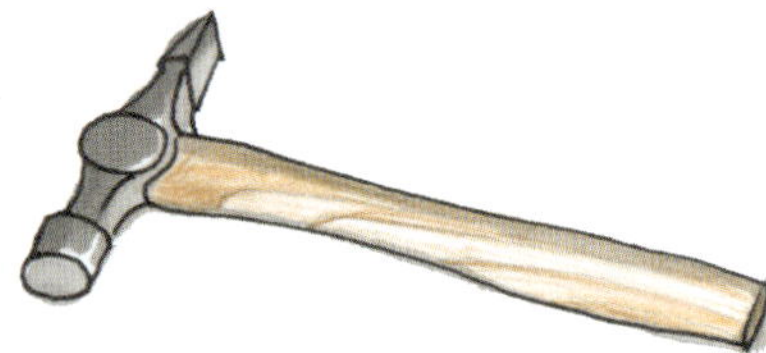

Cross Pein Or Warrington Hammer

A general purpose hammer which gets its name from the wedge-shaped rear face. The wedge is used to start small nails and pins which are held between the fingers.

Ball Pein Hammer

A hammer with a rounded pein at the rear which is used for rounding rivets and other pieces of metal. Ball pein hammers are available in very large sizes for heavy duty work such as hot metalworking.

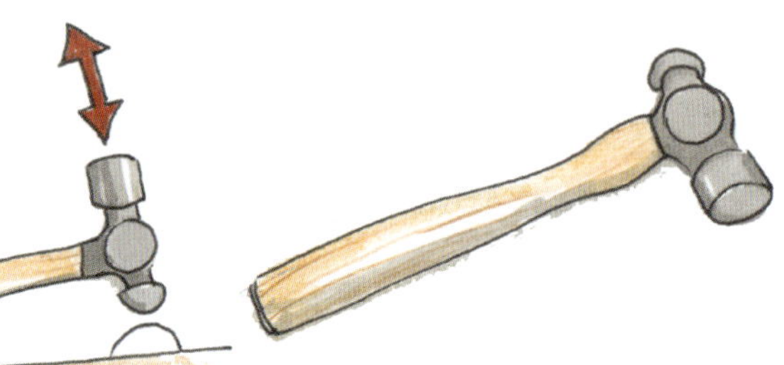

Mallet

Usually made entirely from beech, the mallet is used for driving chisels and gouges and is also used when assembling wooden joints.

Rubber/Nylon Mallet

The modern equivalent of the traditional beech mallet. Can be used for assembling wood joints as well as bending over sheet metals without damaging the surface

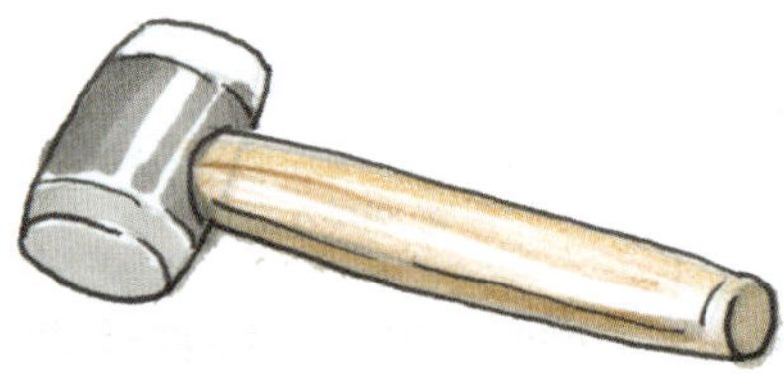

Bossing Mallet

A wooden hammer made with an egg-shaped boxwood head. Used in conjunction with a leather sandbag for hollowing, or dishing, sheet metal.

Planishing Hammer

Has a very polished head which should not be used for general hammering. Used in conjunction with a polished stake for finishing beaten metalwork.

Sheet metal fabrication is extensively used in industry, utilising both hand and machine processes.

Shearing

Cutting sheet metal is usually achieved using a shearing action.

Tinsnips are used to cut small pieces of sheet metal.

Compressed air shears are used in factories to make the task easier.

Bench-mounted shears provide more leverage.

Bending

Bending sheet metal can be done in several ways. Folding bars are one common method although many schools have bending machines.

Pressing

In industry presses are used to bend and form sheet metal. These are controlled by hydraulic rams which create massive pressures. Sheet metal is stamped and pressed cold. Automobile body panels and central heating radiators are two common products which are pressed from sheet steel.

PRESSING FROM HYDRAULIC PRESS

Iron and steel can be heated until it softens. By applying a force from a hammer or press the metal can be reformed. This process is known as forging. Shaping by forging rather than cutting ensures that the grain of the metal is not interrupted. Forged components are therefore much stronger.

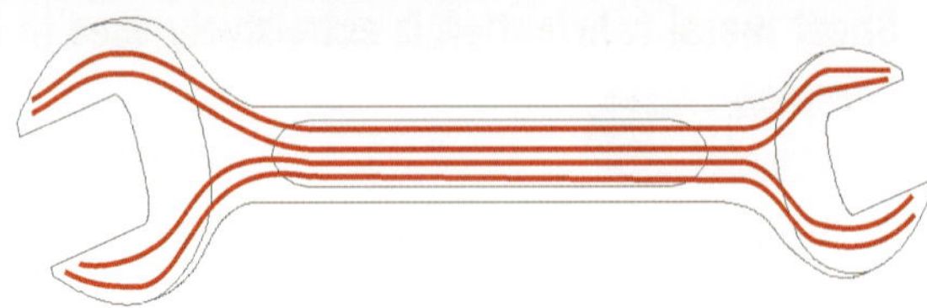

Hand Forging

Traditionally, forging is undertaken by the blacksmith using a hearth to heat the iron or steel and an anvil to withstand the hammer blows. By bending, twisting and hammering a wide variety of forms can be produced.

Drop Forging

Industrially, forging is done by a process called drop or die forging. A large mechanical hammer applies a really large force. The piece of heated metal is placed between two dies and a force is applied in a single blow. Only simple forms can be drop forged.

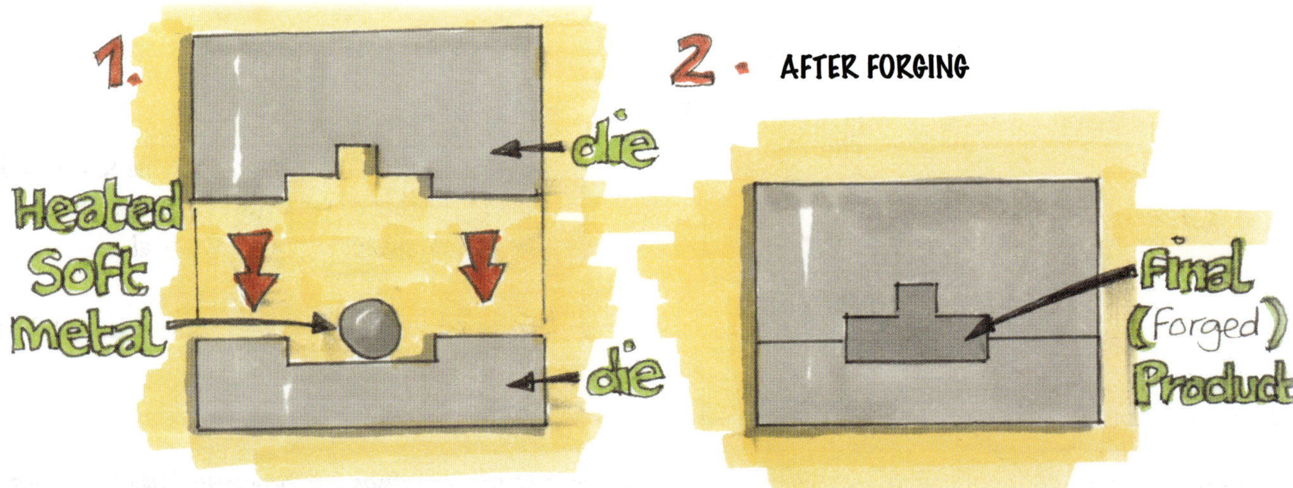

A similar cold forging process is used to stamp out coins and medals. It is appropriately called coining.

In its simplest form, casting involves pouring metal which has been heated and melted into a mould. This is rather like filling a jelly mould.

Split Pattern Sand Casting

Used to form metals such as cast iron, aluminium and brass.

A pattern is made from a timber such as MDF or Jelutong. The pattern is made in two halves and attached to a board.

The pattern is sandwiched between open boxes called a cope and drag.

A special oil-bound sand is used to fill each box. One of the boxes also contains two tapered wooden pegs which will form the pouring spouts.

The pattern is removed and the space left is filled with molten metal.

This method, which is common in schools, is almost identical to the industrial process.

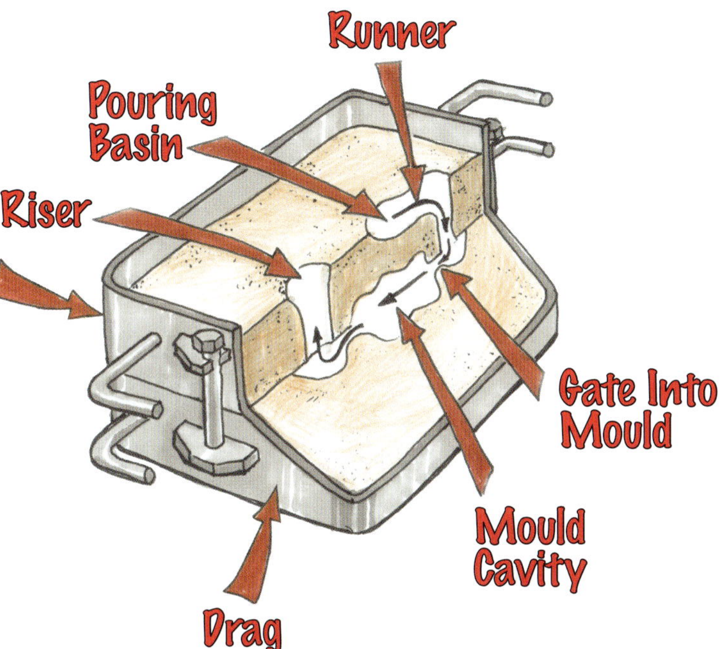

Lost Pattern Casting

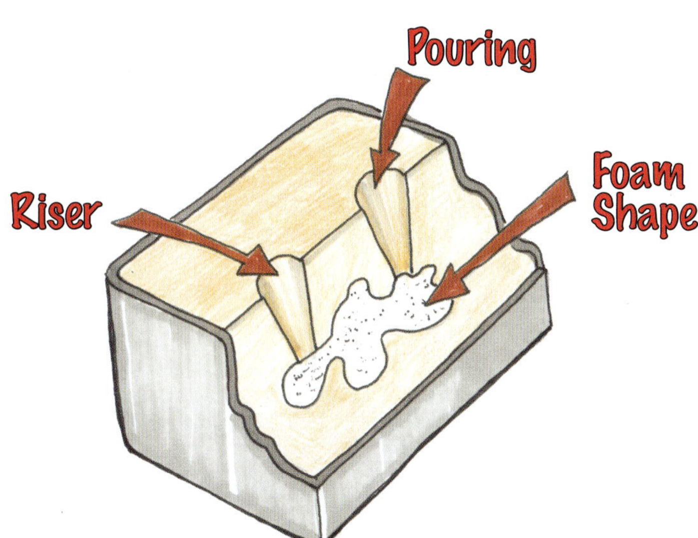

Used to form metals such as aluminium into complete forms which would not be possible with split pattern casting.

A pattern is made from polystyrene foam.

The foam is buried into the sand and pouring spouts and risers added.

The molten metal is poured into the mould and instantly burns away the polystyrene foam, filling the space with molten metal.

Toxic fumes which are produced by this method must be extracted.

A more sophisticated version of this process is used by jewellers to produce rings and brooches. Check out 'lost wax casting'. An even more sophisticated version is used when manufacturing from rapid protoypes. Check out 'stereo lithography'.

Industrial Die Casting

Die casting is very similar to injection moulding and is used to manufacture large quantities of metal products. Alloys which have a lower melting point such as pewter, aluminium alloys and zinc alloys can be used.

The mould is created by spark eroding the form required into two blocks of steel. This mould is water-cooled to control the temperature.

The metal is heated in a crucible until molten.

A hydraulic ram pushes a quantity of the molten metal into the mould.

Pressure is maintained until the metal has cooled enough before the mould is opened.

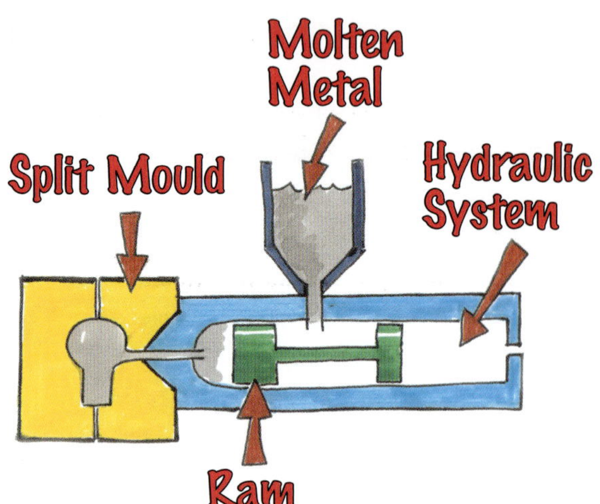

Die Casting In School

Die casting can be replicated in school by using pewter melted with an electric paint stripper gun or a blowlamp. The mould can be machined out of MDF or blocks of high density modelling foam using a CNC milling machine.

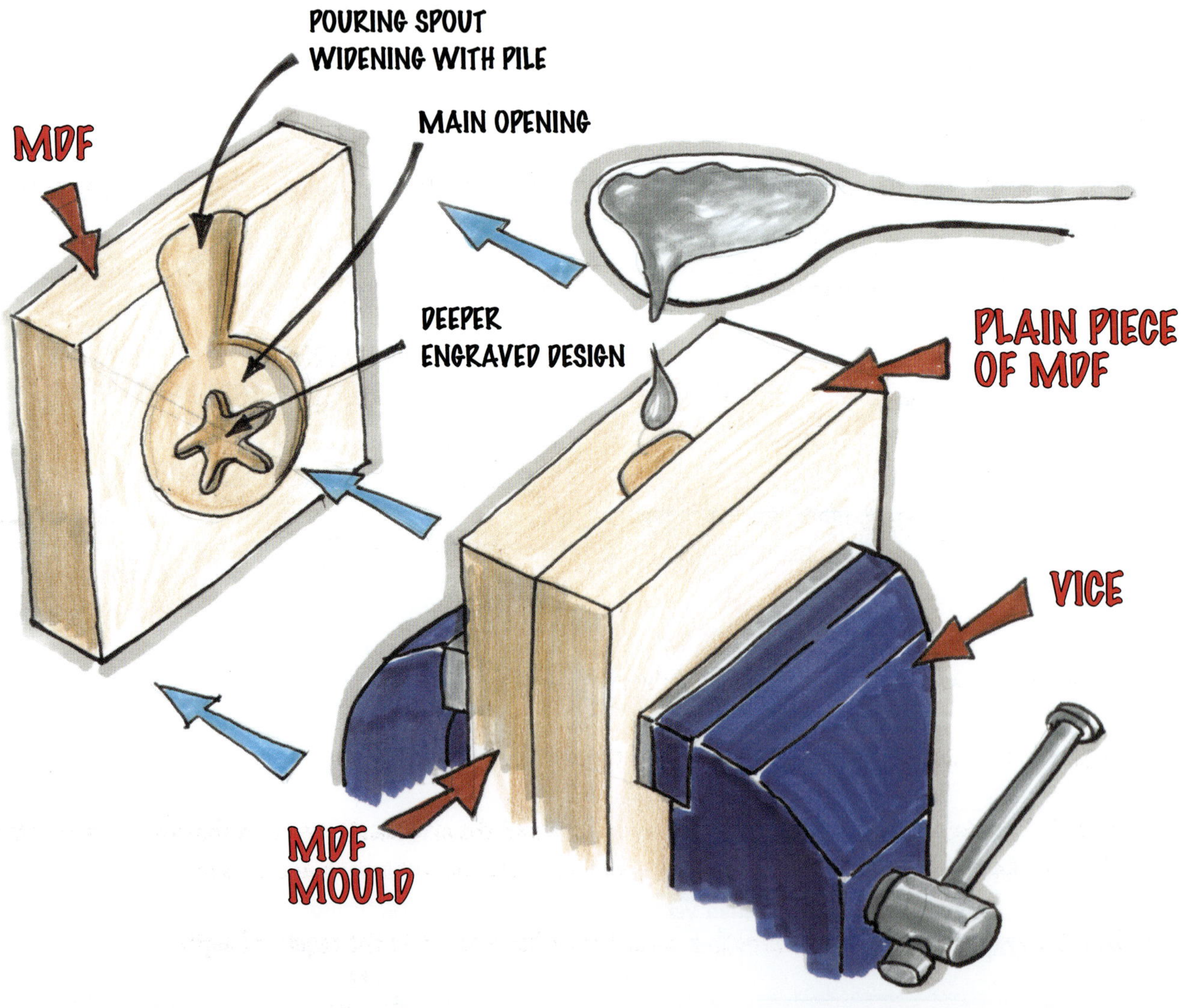

Injection Moulding

Typical Materials used in this process are: POLYTHENE, POLYSTYRENE, POLYPROPYLENE and NYLON.

- Plastic powder or granules are fed from the hopper into a hollow steel barrel.

- The heaters melt the plastic as the screw moves it along towards the mould.

- Once sufficient melted plastic has accumulated, the hydraulic system forces the plastic into the mould.

- Pressure is maintained on the mould, until it has cooled enough to be opened.

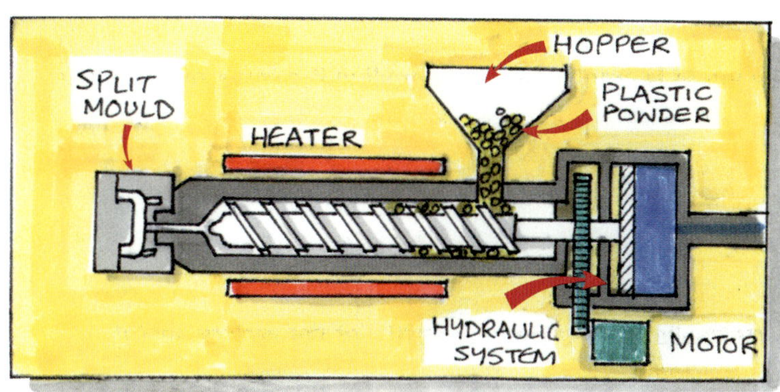

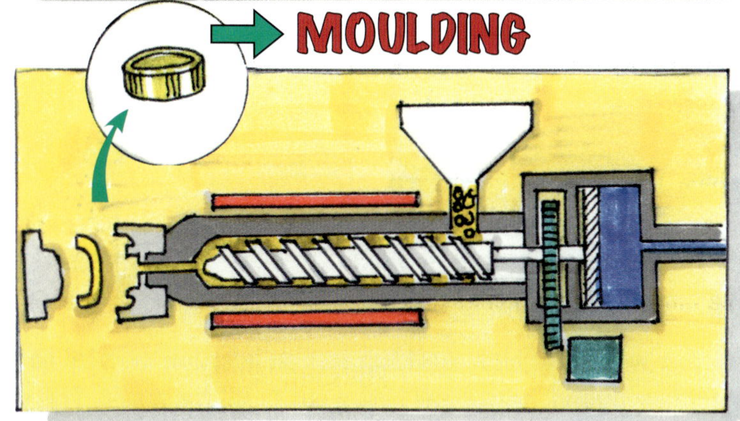

Extrusion

Typical materials used in this process are POLYTHENE, PVC and NYLON. Aluminium alloys can also be extruded although the metal is heated separately.

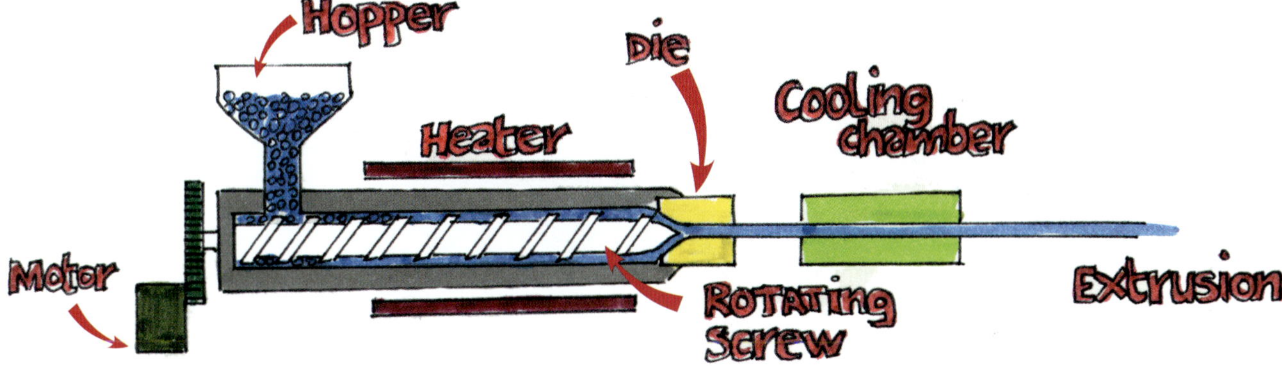

- Plastic granules are fed into the hopper by the rotating screw.

- The plastic granules are heated as they are fed through .

- The difference between the injection moulding process and the extrusion process, is that the softened plastic is forced through a die in a continuous stream, to create long tube or sectional extrusions.

- The extrusions are then passed through a cooling chamber and cut to the required length.

Blow Moulding

Common materials used are PVC, POLYTHENE and POLYPROPYLENE. This process is the same as the EXTRUSION process, apart from the air supply and a split mould instead of the cooling chamber.

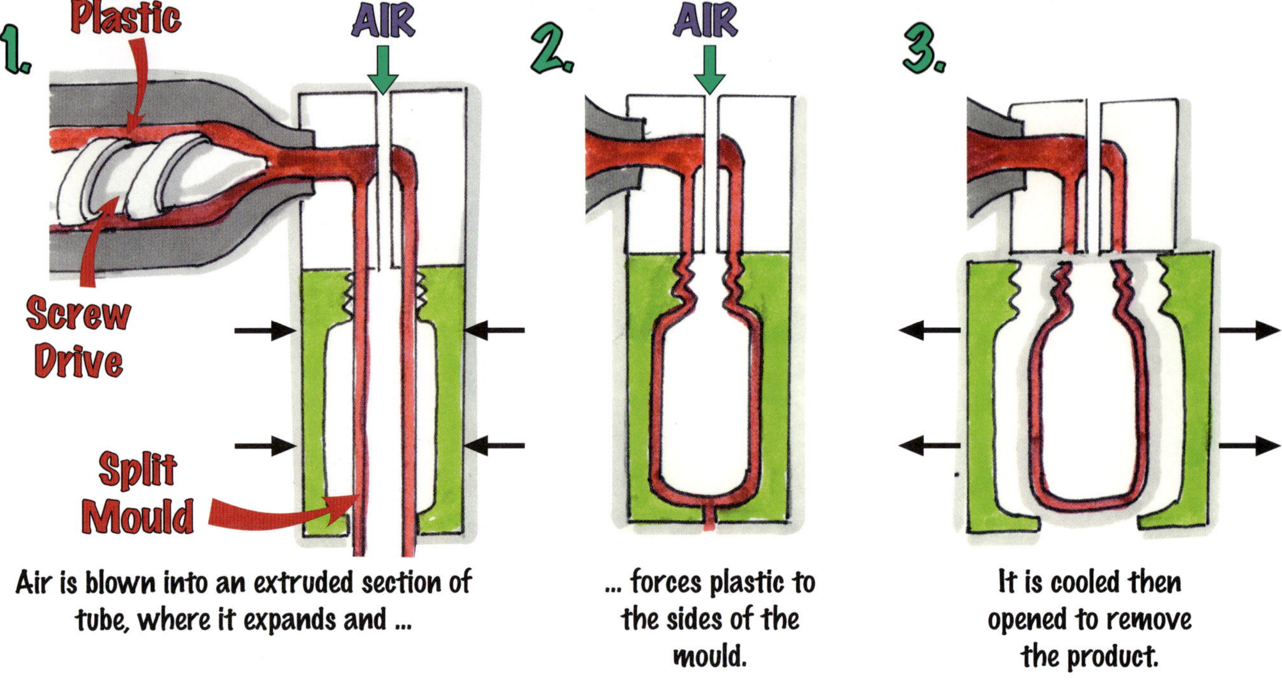

Air is blown into an extruded section of tube, where it expands and ...	... forces plastic to the sides of the mould.	It is cooled then opened to remove the product.

Another method of blow moulding uses an injection moulded bottle blank called a parison. This is clamped around the screw thread, heated and blown out to fill the mould. This method is commonly used for drinks bottles as it keeps the bottle neck thicker and stronger.

Compression Moulding

PHENOL, UREA AND MELAMINE FORMALDEHYDE are materials used in this process.
- A large force is used to squash a cube of polymer into a heated mould.
- The cube of polymer is in the form of a powder, known as a 'slug'.
- Compression moulding is used with THERMOSETTING PLASTICS.

Mould before being heated.	The moulds heat up and are pressed together ...	... to form the final product.

Rotational Moulding

This process can be used as an alternative to INJECTION or BLOW moulding. Mould costs are very much cheaper, (by up to 90%). It is easier to make alterations to a rotational mould, cutting down the development time in manufacture. A rotational mould machine has three arms fixed at the same point. Moulds would be attached to each arm and rotated continuously with thermoplastic powder.

- Used to make footballs, road cones and storage tanks.
- Mouldings are made from POLYTHENE (PE) - which has fire retardant and vandal resistant qualities.

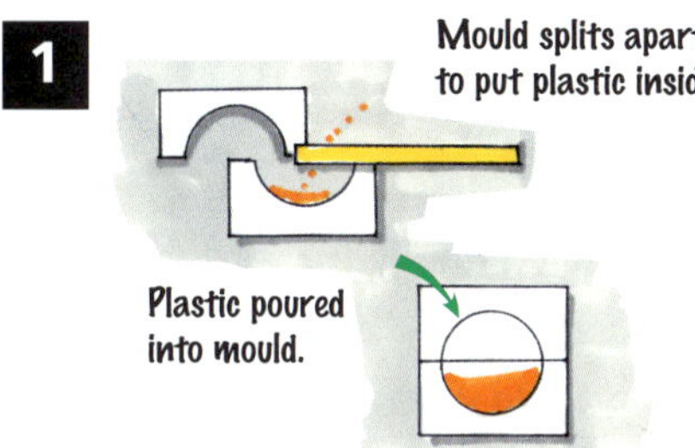

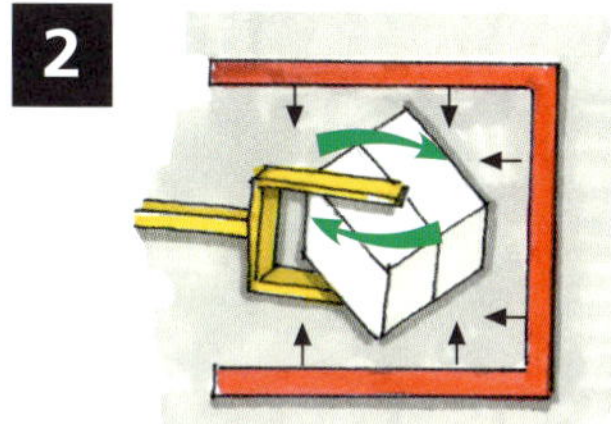

Vacuum Forming

This technique uses thermoplastic materials in the form of sheets which can measure up to 1.5m x 1.8m. Perhaps the most popular material is High Impact Polystyrene (H.I.P.S.) which is cheap and easy to form. Basically the process relies on 'sucking' heated plastic onto the shape of mould that is required.

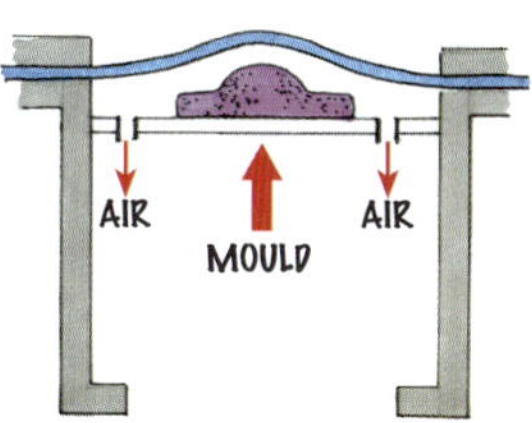

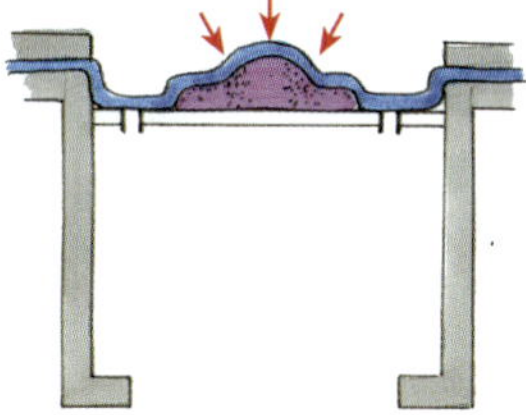

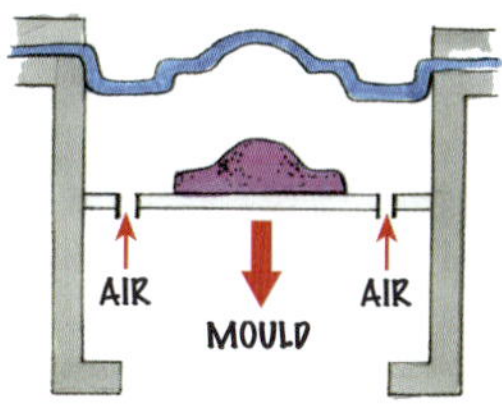

- The plastic is heated and the mould moves close to it.
- Air is 'sucked out' to form a vacuum.

- Removing the air causes the hot plastic to be sucked onto the mould.
- As the temperature of the plastic falls, a rigid impression of the mould is formed.

- The vacuum pump is turned off, allowing air to enter
- The mould is lowered, separating it from the final product.

Line Bending

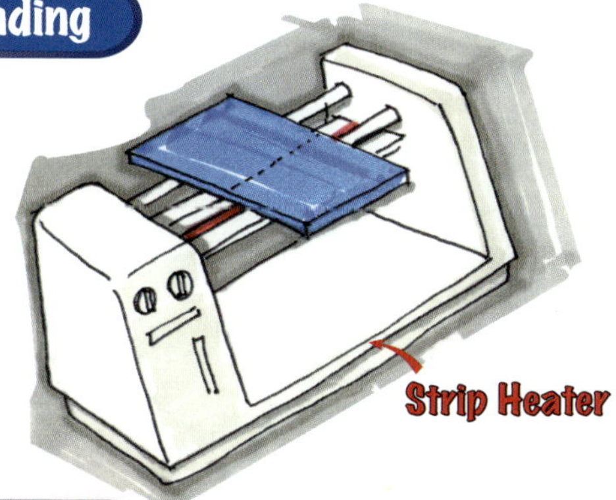

- Again, thermoplastic sheets are used in this technique, but this time they are heated only along the line of the intended fold, by a special heating element.
- Temperature switches control the amount of heat produced to cater for different thicknesses of material.
- Acrylic sheets are often used for this process, and bending jigs can be used to produce accurate angles, and shapes.

SAFETY TIP
Keep your fingers away from the heat element and always remember to switch off after use.

There are many traditional joints which can be used to build structural strength into products (and further research may be needed in this area.) The following are a small selection of those commonly used in schools.

Butt Joint

Simple but weak. Can be mitred which is often used in picture frames.

Mortise And Tenon

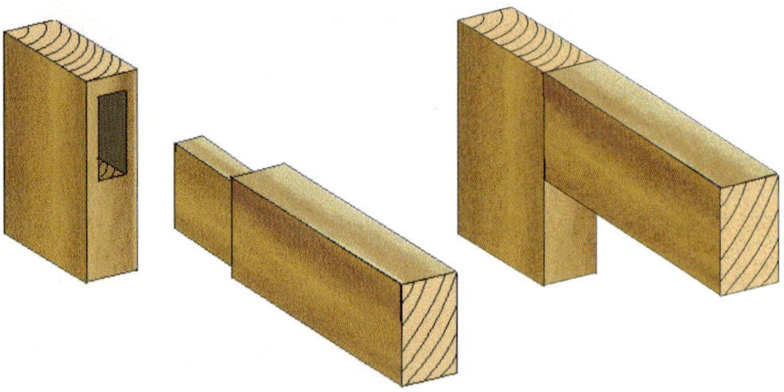

A strong joint. It is easy to remember the names of each part as tools are named after them - tenon saw, mortise chisel. In commercial production the mortise is milled out so the tenon is machined with a rounded edge.

Lap Joint

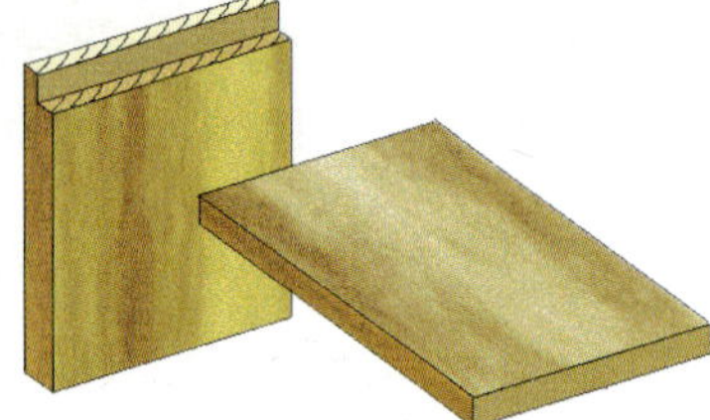

A little stronger than butt joints as there is a bigger surface area for gluing. Often strengthened with nails.

Dovetail

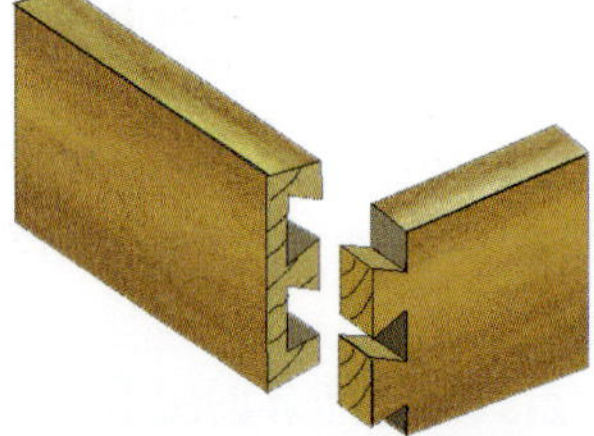

The strongest joint for box constructions in natural timber. Look very decorative but can be very difficult to cut by hand using a saw and chisel. Jigs are available for using a special dovetail cutter in a router.

Halving Joint

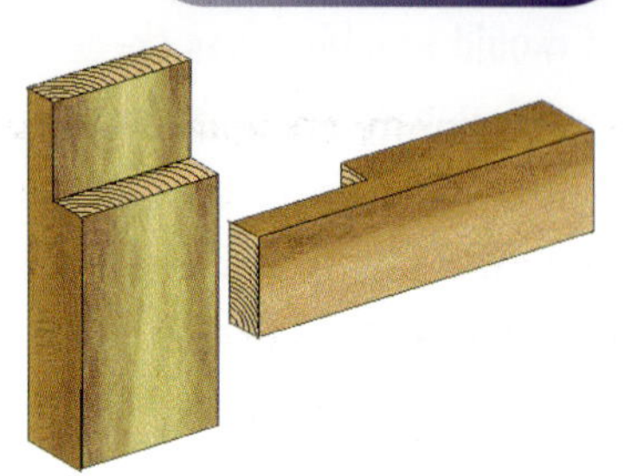
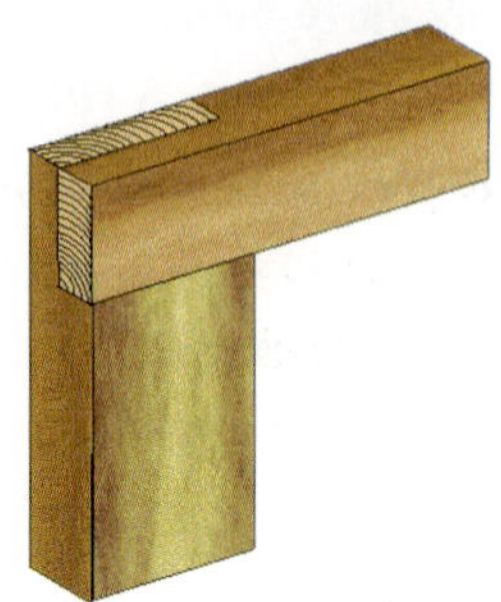

There are several variations on this joint which involves removing half the material from each piece using a saw and chisel. Sometimes strengthened with a dowel through the joint.

Dowel Joint

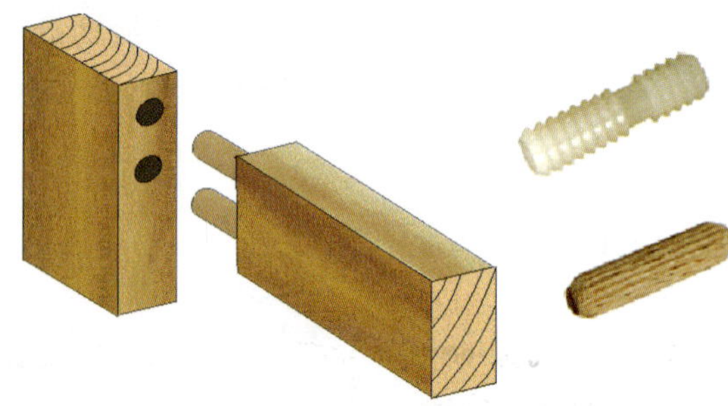

Very easy to produce and is popular in commercial production as it relies on aligned holes and pegs (dowels). Some commercial products use serrated plastic dowels for home assembly.

Housing Joint

A simple slot is cut into one piece to increase the glue area. Often done with an electrically powered router and is especially effective with MDF.

In commercial production traditional wood joints are being replaced with new methods which are quicker to produce and often stronger. The trend towards many products being produced in flat-pack form has increased this trend.

Nails

A very weak joint which gets slightly stronger as they rust inside the timber. Used with glue, nailed joints are often used for fixing backs of cupboards, decorative mouldings and general building and DIY work. Many different types of nail are available.

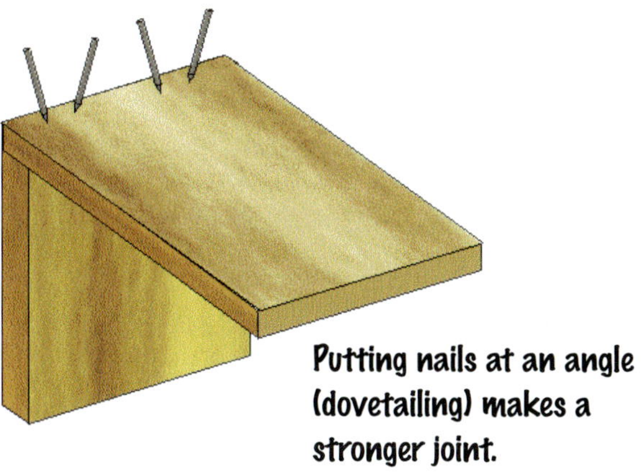

Putting nails at an angle (dovetailing) makes a stronger joint.

Screws

Often combined with glue. Can be very strong when used across the grain. Lots of different types available but a massive increase in cross head screws as they are easier to drive in by hand or using an electrically powered driver. Useful for fixing other materials, such as metals or plastics to timber.

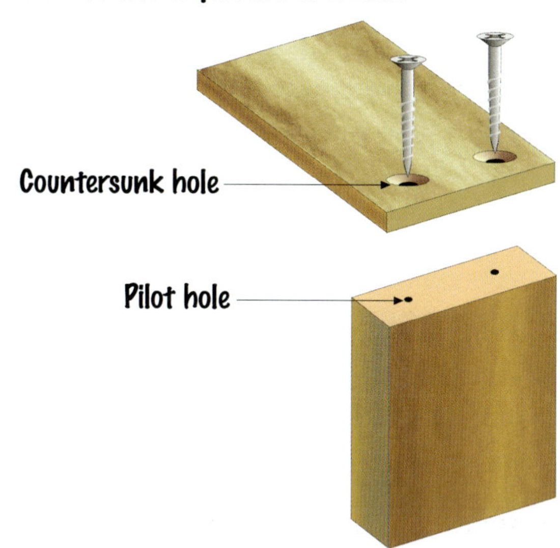

Knock-down Fittings

A massive range of knock-down fittings are now available to satisfy both the DIY and commercial production markets.

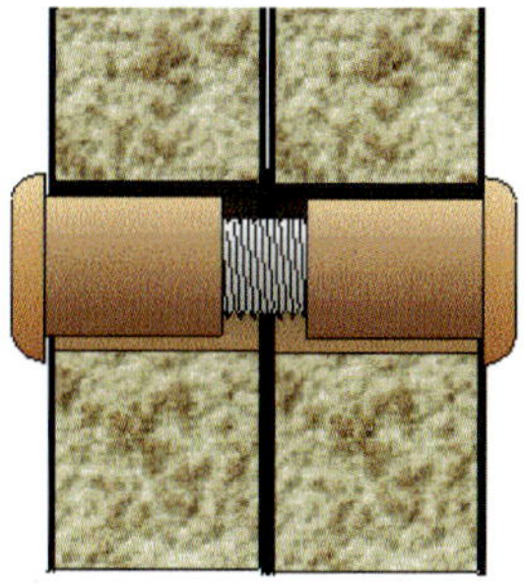

Cabinet screws. Used to join kitchen units together.

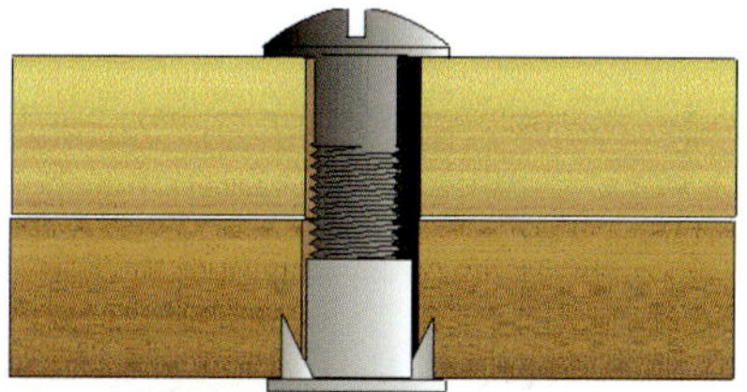

Pronged nut. Really useful if you want to take apart again. Simply taps into a hole to provide a threaded insert which will take a range of machine screws.

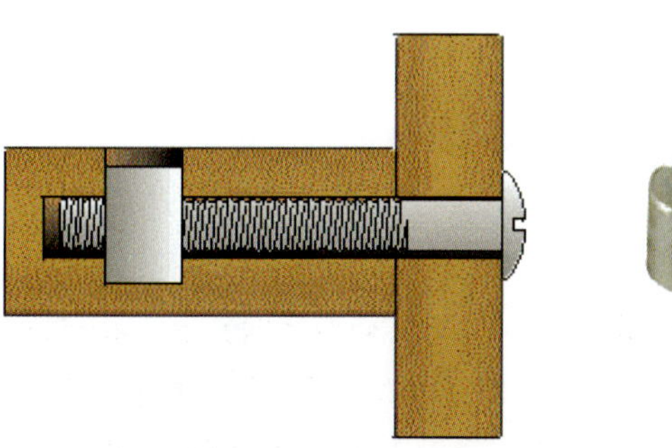

Cross dowel. A metal-screwed insert which sits in a hole and takes a range of machine screws. It is very strong indeed.

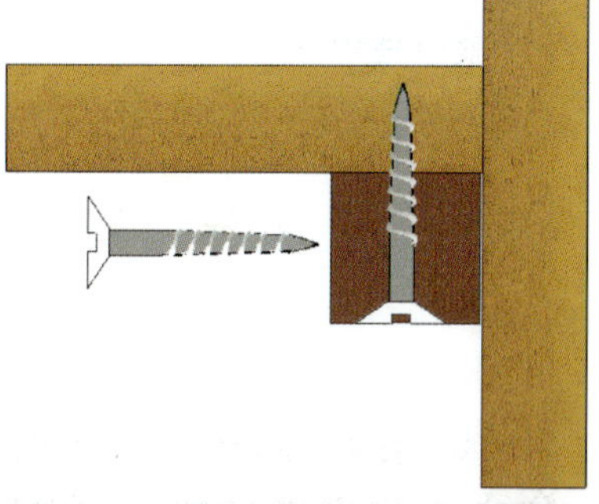

Block joints are available in a range of colours. These plastic blocks are simply used to take screws in each direction. They are suitable for simple box joints.

Metals can be joined using heat and a bonding alloy to form a permanent joint. The most common methods are soft soldering, hard soldering and welding.

Soldering

SOFT SOLDERING

Soft soldering is a method of joining metal parts together using a lead based alloy. Flux is applied to the joint and heated using a gas torch or metal soldering bit. Soft soldering is used for light applications such as electrical connections and plumbing joints.

HARD SOLDERING

The most common version called brazing is used for heavier applications as the joint is much stronger. The brass bonding alloy (or spelter) melts at a much higher temperature than soft soldering. A borax flux is mixed to a paste with water and applied to the join. This is then heated to an orange colour with a gas torch at which point the spelter will melt around the join. This method is most commonly used for joining mild steel but copper can also be brazed.

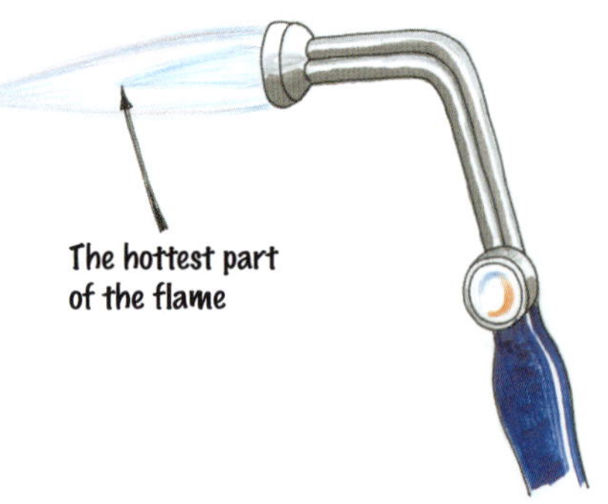

SILVER SOLDERING

Silver soldering is an almost identical process to brazing but a silver based alloy is used. Silver soldering is used on brass, copper and guilding metal as the bonding alloy melts at a lower temperature than brazing spelter.

Welding

Several methods are used to melt a pool of the metals being joined together with the bonding alloy.

GAS WELDING

Gas welding involves using a torch to heat up the joint. A mixture of acetylene gas and oxygen produces a very small hot flame which melts both the filler rod and the surrounding metal. Gas welding equipment is extremely dangerous and should not be used by anyone other than especially trained staff in schools.

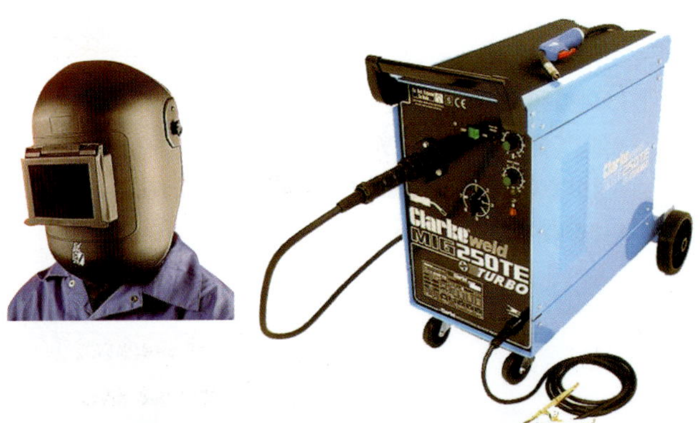

MIG WELDING

MIG welding is most commonly used in schools. An electrical spark creates the heat. The area is cooled with a gas mixture of argon and carbon dioxide. The spark also creates a very bright light which will damage eyesight so a protective facemask must be used when welding. MIG is one form of electric arc welding and is often used in production welding using robots.

SPOT WELDING

Spot welding is one form of resistance welding and is used for melting thin sheet steel together such as car bodies. Electrodes, usually made of copper, sandwich the metal together and a current is passed between them. The resistance creates the heat to bond the two metals in a tiny spot. Wheels can be used to do a similar process called seam welding. Spot welding is especially suitable for use with robot arms as the process is so easy to control.

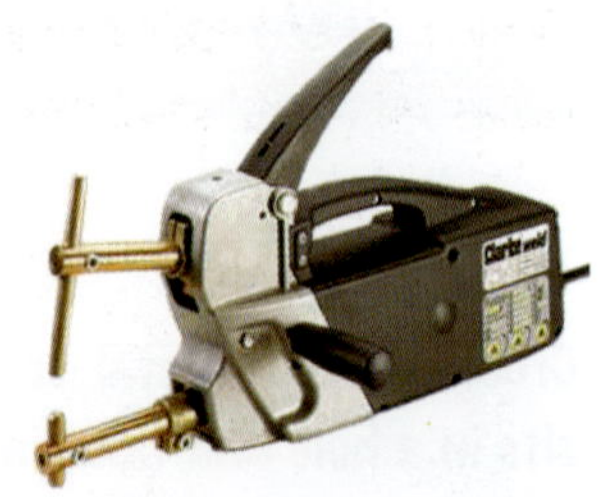

Metals are often permanently joined using thermal methods. Mechanical joining methods have the advantage of being able to join dissimilar metals (and indeed other materials to metals). Some plastics can be thermally bonded although adhesives are more often used. The following methods can be used with both metals and plastics.

Nuts And Bolts

There are numerous variations on this system of joining. Threads are sometimes cut into one piece of the material.

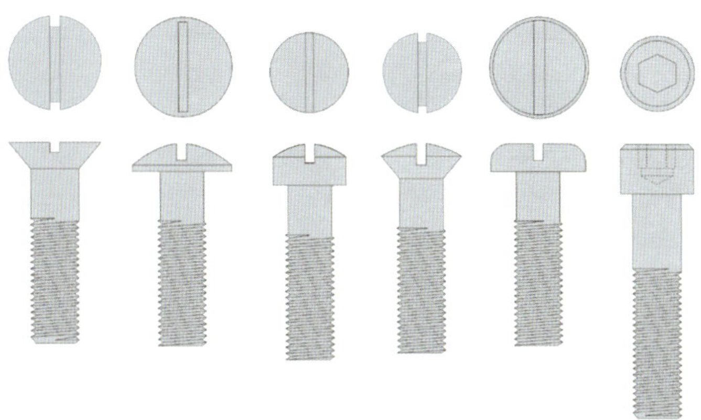

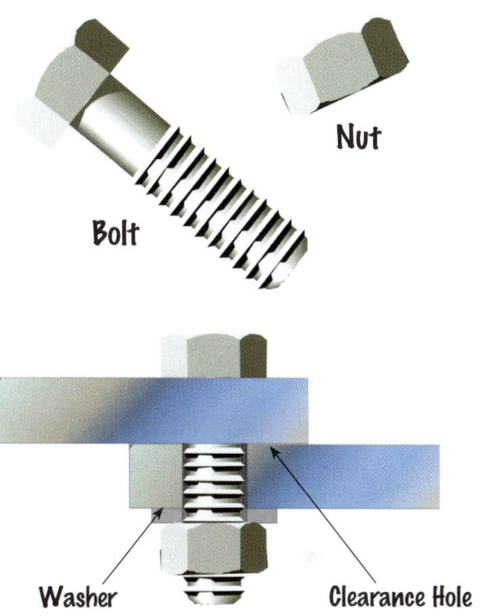

Bolts are made with many different heads. Threads also vary although metric threads are now almost standard in schools - M3 to M12 being the most popular. Available in many lengths, typically 20mm - 100mm. Smaller bolts are called machine screws and have the thread over the entire length.

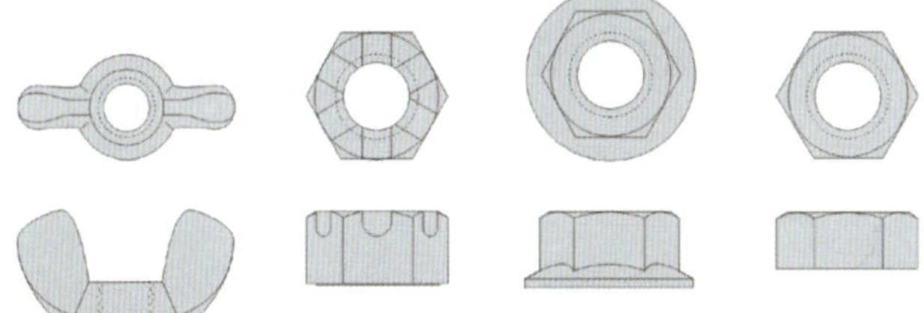

A washer is usually used under the nut. This might be a plain ring, or sprung, to keep the nut from vibrating loose.

Nuts must obviously match the same thread as the bolt and so they also come in a variety of types. Wing nuts are tightened by hand and are useful for more temporary joints. Hexagonal heads are tightened with a spanner.

Rivets

Rivets are a more permanent joining method than nuts and bolts. Rivets work on forming a head on both sides of the materials being joined. The traditional method is to hammer the blank end of the rivet to form a second head. Nowadays, pop rivets are a much more common method.

A variety of heads are available. Rivets are most often made from soft mild steel, copper or aluminium.

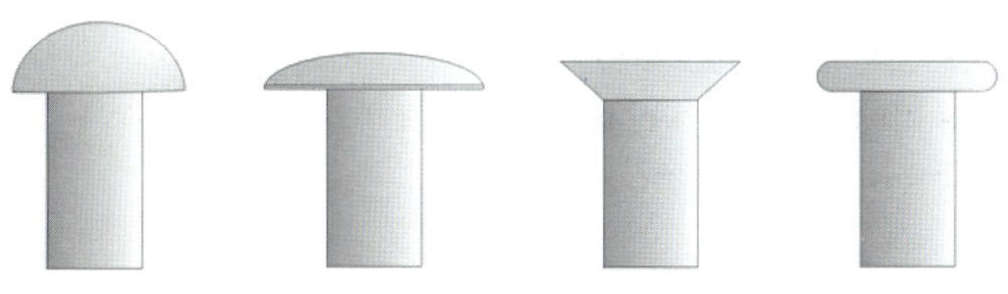

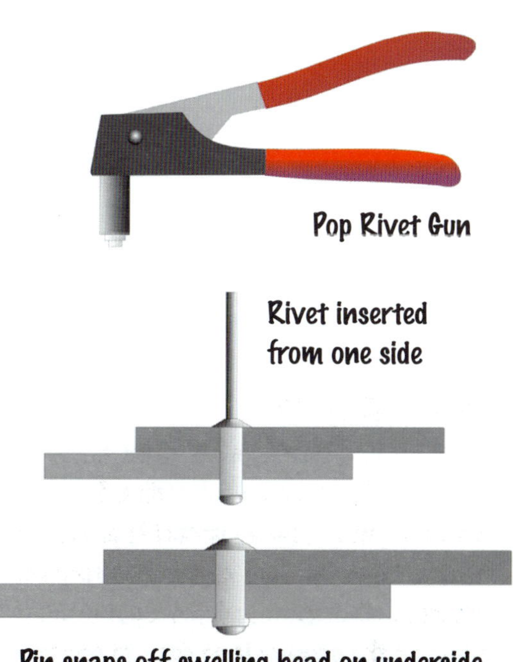

Screw cutting can be carried out on most metals, some plastics and indeed even some hardwoods although the latter is a very specialised task usually restricted to the toy-making industry.

Tapping

Internal, or female, threads are usually cut with a tap. This is a very hard steel tool which makes its own thread as it is twisted into the material.

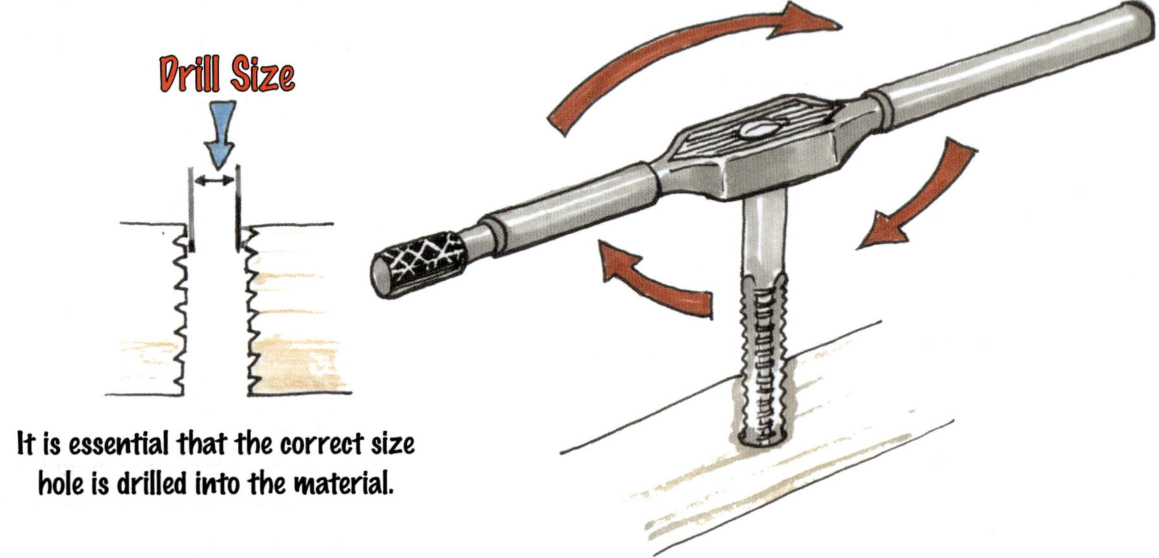

It is essential that the correct size hole is drilled into the material.

A tap wrench is used to turn the tap.

Threading

This is the cutting of an external, or male, thread. The tool used is called a split die and is held in a die stock so that it can be turned.

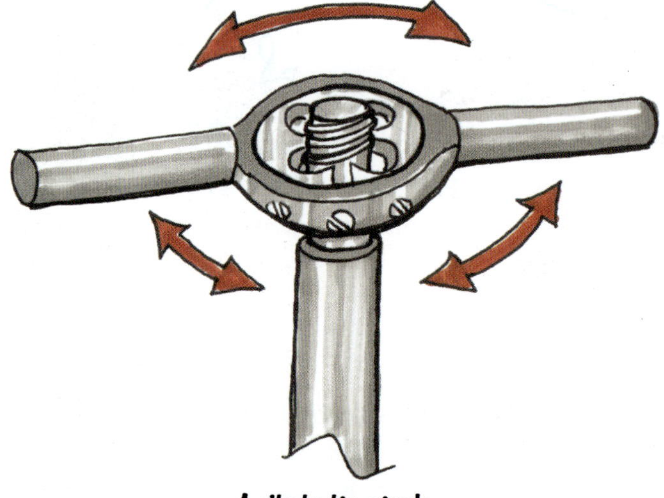

A die in its stock

Cutting A Thread On A Lathe

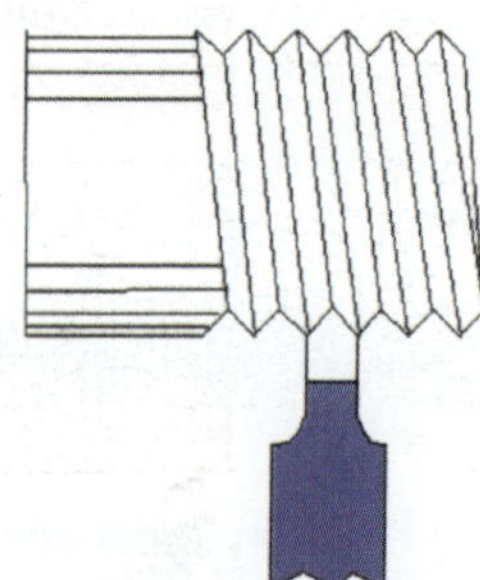

Threading can be cut with a lathe. In industry, many threads are rolled; hard-threaded rollers rotate the material and press it into shape. This is a form of cold forging. Plastic threads are usually injection moulded.

Adhesives work on several different principles. There are many specialist adhesives manufactured for specific purposes.

PVA

Polyvinyl Acetate is a white water-based adhesive. The PVA soaks into the surface and sets once the water is absorbed into the wood. It is often regarded as being stronger than the wood fibres themselves and so makes a very strong bond.

Synthetic Resin

A waterproof adhesive which needs to be mixed into a creamy consistency with water. Chemical hardening takes place. Very hard and brittle. Will set in the plumbing outlet so do not wash residue down the sink!

Solvent Cement

There are several types available. The most common is Dichloromethane which works by dissolving the surface of hard plastics such as Acrylic and High Impact Polystyrene. Very dangerous fumes are given off so ventilation is essential.

Hot Melt Glue

The use of glue guns are common in schools. Hot melt glue is useful for quick modelling but can rarely be used in final products.

Epoxy Resin

A very versatile but expensive adhesive which will stick most clean dry materials. Equal amounts of resin and hardener are mixed together. Chemically sets to a very hard material.

Contact Adhesive

Both surfaces are coated and allowed to become touch-dry. Adhesion takes place as soon as the two surfaces meet. The solvent fumes are very dangerous and good ventilation is essential.

Latex Adhesive

A rubber solution which is cheap and very safe. Does not give off any dangerous fumes although the smell is not pleasant.

The chart opposite offers some initial guidance but it is always worth testing out samples first, especially when sticking plastics.

	FABRIC	PLASTICS	METALS	WOOD
WOOD	PVA	CONTACT ADHESIVE	CONTACT ADHESIVE	PVA OR SYNTHETIC RESIN
METALS	CONTACT ADHESIVE	CONTACT ADHESIVE	EPOXY RESIN	CONTACT ADHESIVE
PLASTICS	CONTACT ADHESIVE	SOLVENT CEMENT	EPOXY RESIN	CONTACT ADHESIVE
FABRIC	LATEX ADHESIVE	CONTACT ADHESIVE	CONTACT ADHESIVE	PVA

Accuracy is an important part of your coursework assessment and it is hard to imagine any manufactured product which doesn't require some degree of measuring. It is also important to check key measurements, especially where parts need to fit together.

Steel Rule

A generally more accurate measuring tool than a stationery rule. The zero point begins at the end of the rule so you can measure more accurately from the end of a piece of material. Millimetres are used in D&T not centimetres - ie. 200mm not 20cm.

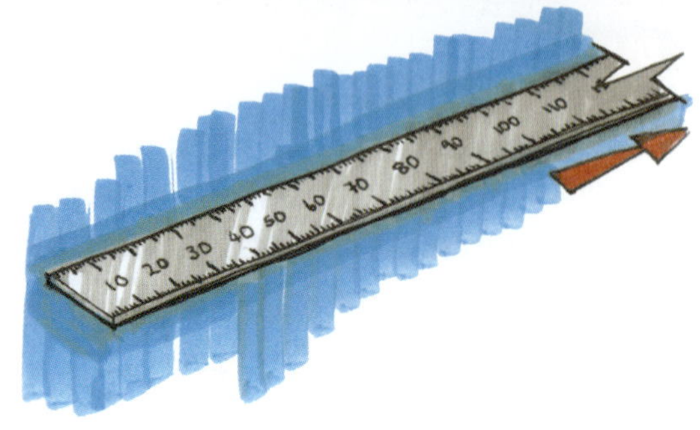

Steel Tape Measure

An essential aid when working on larger-sized materials. The lip at the end of the tape slides to allow you to measure from the end of the material or against a raised surface.

Calipers

Used to measure the outside or the inside of circular bars and tubes. When pulled across the surface of the material they should feel as if you are dragging a magnet. Not accurate enough for real precision tasks but suitable when adhesives are being used or soldering is taking place.

Micrometer

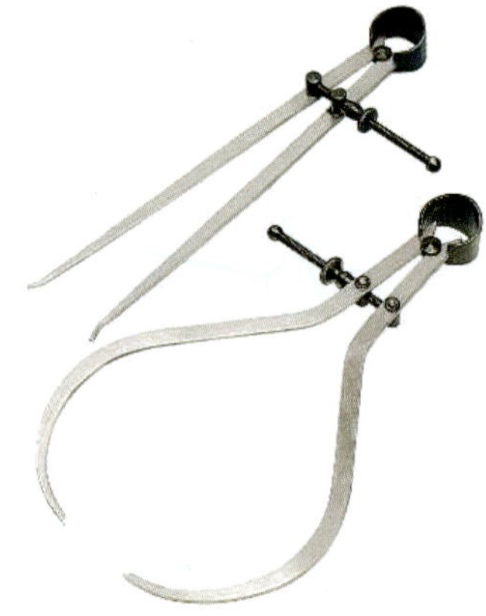

Although it is only capable of measuring outside dimensions it is accurate up to 0.01mm. A ratchet mechanism prevents the jaws being pressed too hard. Micrometers are available only for a given range, for example 0 - 50mm, 50mm - 100mm.

Vernier Gauge

Very accurate for measuring both inside and outside dimensions. The latest digital versions are probably the most accurate measuring tools available to you.

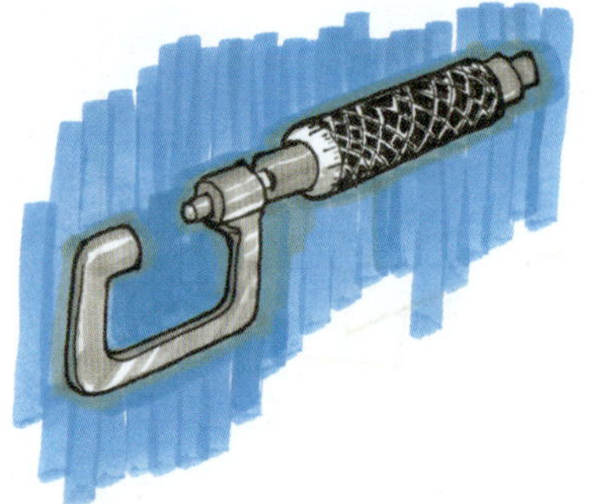

Spirit Level

A tool for checking horizontal and vertical surfaces. The bubble in the tube must fall within the markings. Especially useful when fitting shelves, for example.

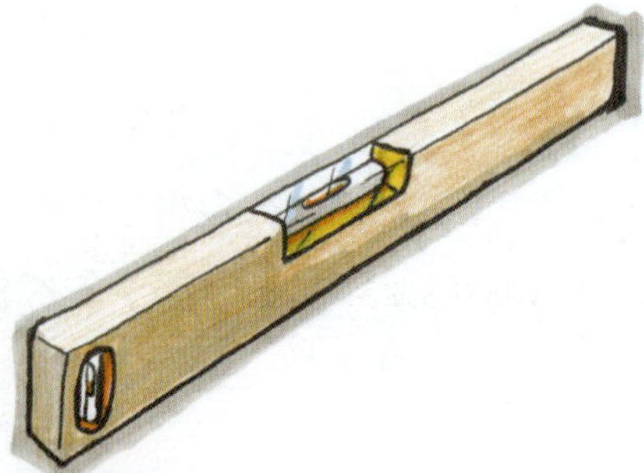

You might need to manufacture many identical items, for example parts of a child's construction set. To ensure that each part is identical you will need to undertake some form of measuring checks. This might be one part of your quality assurance procedures.

Any of the tools listed on the previous page might be used to check measurements. However, making a special tool is often easier if lots of identical measurements are needed.

Measuring Stick

A simple cut length of material can be used to check lengths. If cut with pointed ends it is especially useful for checking that diagonals on a box are the same (therefore the box is square).

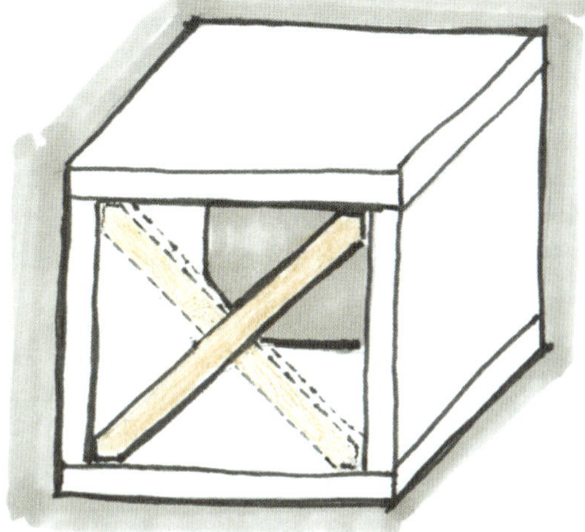

Gap Gauge

Another simple checking tool that can easily be made to ensure that components are the correct size.

Try Square

Used as a checking device to ensure materials are accurately cut and sanded to right angles. Also used for checking that structures, such as jewellery boxes, have been assembled square.

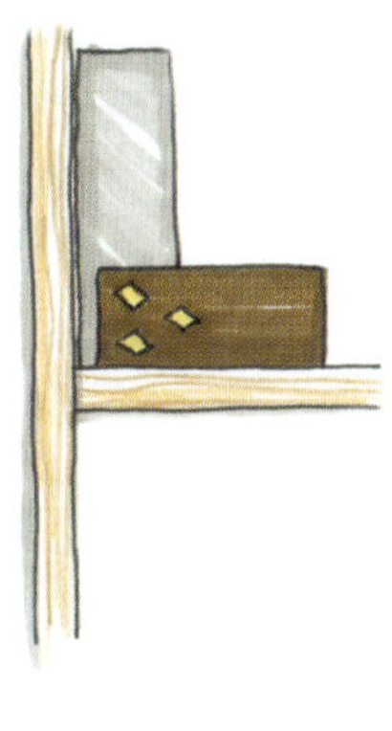

Even Vernier Gauges and micrometers are not accurate enough for many manufacturing industries who use sophisticated technologies such as lasers and ultrasonics to measure and check dimensions. Check this out on the Internet.
Try searching for:

Laser measuring devices
Laser profilometry
3D microscopy
Ultrasonic measuring

Many materials need some form of surface finish to enhance them visually and also to protect them from deterioration. Surface finishes can be applied by a variety of methods including brushing and spraying.

Paints

Paints can be used on metals or timber but are generally unsuitable for plastics (although there are some specialist paints available for plastics). They can be grouped into three main categories:

1. Oil-based Paints

Oil-based paints usually produce gloss finishes. Durable and suitable for both metals and timber. It is important to prime the material before applying the paint. A good brush or roller is essential. Clean up with turps substitute or white spirit. Most modern oil-based paints are suitable for use on children's toys and can be used internally or externally.

2. Water-based Paints

Water-based paints are available in a wide range of finishes from matt to high gloss. There has been a big increase in the availability of water-based paints in recent years. Some are only suitable for light use such as on walls eg. matt vinyl emulsion. Generally suitable for use on timbers although some are available for metals. Not as durable as oil-based paints. Clean up with warm water and plenty of detergent.

3. Solvent-based Paints

Solvent-based paints dry much quicker than other types and are usually available in spray cans. Although brush-on varieties are available, they are difficult to apply. These paints include a range of interesting finishes such as hammered, crackle etc. These paints are generally more expensive but can give better results on small products. The correct solvent (often cellulose based) is needed for cleaning up. Good ventilation is essential as these vapours are toxic and a big fire risk!

Varnishes And Lacquers

These are available in oil, water and solvent-based forms. Varnishes are clear or translucent and are available in matt, satin or gloss finishes. Spray cans are particularly suitable for small products and there are versions available which have been developed especially for coating metals.

Oil

Teak and similar timbers are naturally oily. The application of teak oil or linseed oil will provide a finish which improves the appearance of the grain of the wood and protects it for outdoor use. Vegetable oil can be applied to timbers which are going to come into contact with food eg. salad servers.

French Polish

A traditional finish which is achieved by dissolving shellac in methylated spirits. Applied by brush and cloth the finish is built up in layers to achieve a very deep finish. Wax is usually applied on top of the French Polish to enhance the shine.

Wood Stains

Wood stains can be used to enhance the colour of the timber and show up the grain patterns. Stains are available in almost every colour but can only be used effectively if they are darker than the natural timber. On their own they are not really considered as a surface finish as they require an additional coating of wax or varnish to protect the timber from moisture penetration. Stains are available in water or solvent-based forms and can also be supplied as stained varnishes. They are usually applied with a cloth.

Sanding Sealer

Usually a solvent-based product similar to a varnish which is used to seal timber. The quick drying liquid seals the surface and raises the fibres of the timber so they can be cut back with fine abrasive paper. Suitable as a first coat before applying varnish or wax polish. Works well on top of wood stains.

Plastic Dip-coating

Polythene is the most common thermoplastic powder which is used for this process. Air is blown through the powder to make it behave like a liquid. Metal, pre-heated to 180 degrees is dipped in the fluidised powder and returned to the oven where it melts to form a smooth finish. Commercially used for products such as dishwasher racks, it is often used on school projects for coat hooks and tool handles.

Powder Coating

Powder coating is an industrial finish which is a more sophisticated version of dip-coating. The powder is sprayed onto the products which flow through an oven. Modern powder coating provides a paint-like finish and is available in all colours as well as translucent. It is extremely durable.

Anodising

Anodising is a process used on aluminium to provide a durable corrosion-resistant finish. It involves electrolysis and uses acids and electric currents which are hazardous in school workshops. Colour can be added to tint the aluminium. Most common finishing process used on aluminium.

Plating

Plating is another process which uses electrolysis. There are many forms although chromium plating is the most widely recognised. The thin layer of metal on the surface provides a durable finish on metals which are prone to corrosion.

Galvanising

Galvanising involves dipping metal (usually mild steel) into a bath of molten zinc. The zinc provides a really corrosion resistant finish although not the most attractive.

Self-finishing

Many products are self-finished. This is true for instance, of injection moulded products. It is the mould which is highly polished which ensures that the same surface is transferred onto each product.

Polishing is a very common finishing method used on timbers, metals and hard plastics such as acrylic.

Polishing Timber

On timber it is usual to use a wax polish. This may be applied by hand using a cloth or it may be applied using a buffing wheel. Polish fills the porous surface of the timber and a layer of polish is built up on the surface of the material.

There are various types of polish suitable for timber including beeswax and silicone polish.

Polishing Metals

Metal polish is always slightly abrasive as it relies on cutting away the surface of the metal until it is very smooth. Metal polishes can be in liquid form or in a wax bar which is applied to a buffing wheel.

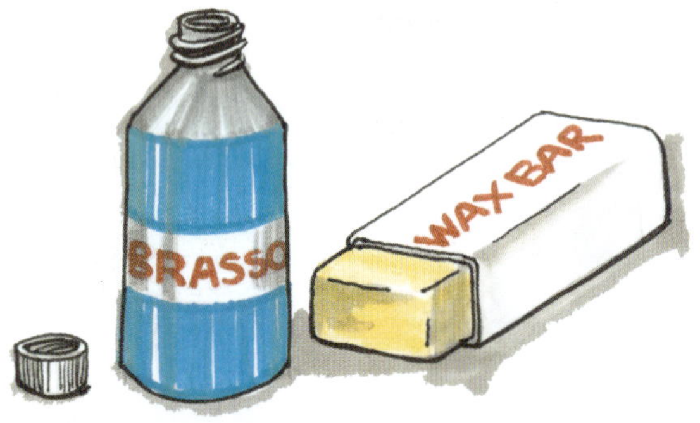

POLISH MACHINE WITH TWO BUFFING WHEELS

Polishing Plastics

Hard plastics such as acrylic are often polished on their cut edges and polishing can also be used to remove fine scratches. This is usually achieved by using a metal polish applied by hand with a cloth or using a buffing wheel. Polishing compounds, such as Vonax, allow a high gloss surface to be achieved. However, it is easy to overheat the edge of the plastic, by pressing too hard onto the buffing wheel, which can permanently damage the surface.

BAR RUBBED ON BUFFING MOP

WORK PUSHED ONTO MOP

There are several different types of systems and controls which you need to understand and use.

Systems

A system is made up of three main parts - Input, Process and Output. Systems are often made up of lots of sub-systems. Many of the systems you will use also have feedback loops in them. These terms will appear in all of the systems you study.

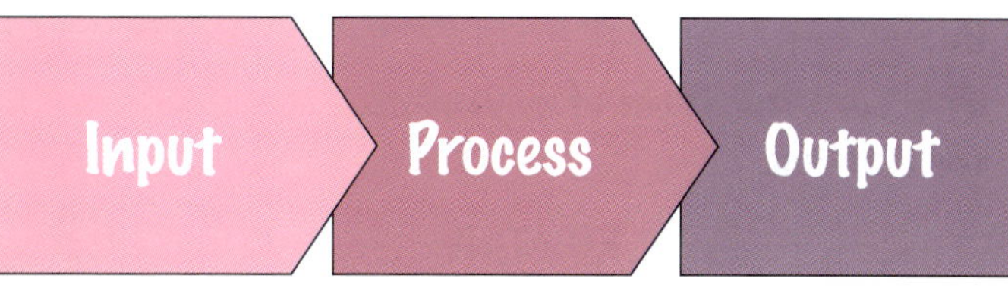

Mechanical Systems

Inputs are described in terms of the movements they make. The following pages describe these in more detail and suggest some processes which can be used to create the desired output. Mechanical systems control movement ensuring that the input, which might well be an electric motor, is turned into a useful output such as a cutting action on a power hacksaw.

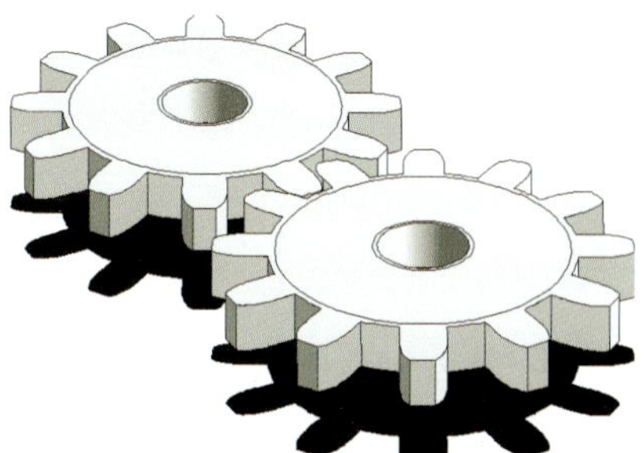

Production Systems

Inputs are the raw materials at the start of the operation and outputs are the components or whole products which are manufactured. Production systems control all the processes of manufacturing including the organisation of materials, workforce and plant (the machines and equipment used). Many sub-systems can be found in even the smallest factory.

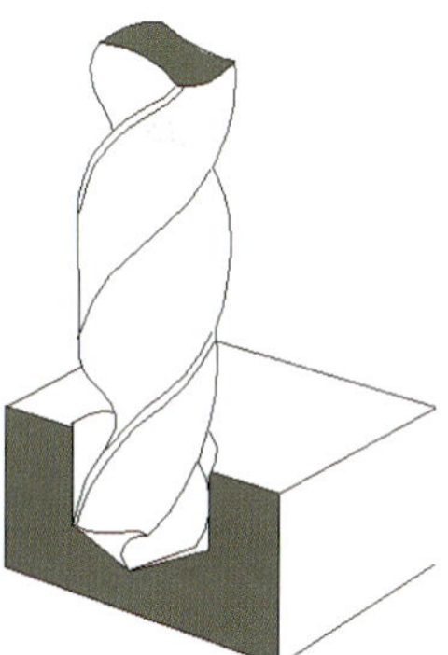

Quality Assurance Systems

Any manufacturing system is only as good as its Quality Assurance procedures. The inputs might be a combination of materials, mechanical systems and production processes. Quality Assurance provides the feedback loops which are such a necessary part of manufacturing. It involves defining when checks have to be made, exactly how the checks will take place and what action (feedback) will be necessary. Quality Assurance and the Quality Control checks which are needed in such a system are described in more detail later in this section.

Health And Safety Systems

It is vital that Health & Safety is taken into account at every stage of a product's life. The required output is the safety of everyone involved in the manufacturing of a product and in its safe use and eventual disposal. The input relies on everyone involved taking an active part in the overall process. Feedback is essential, whether it is simply a case of telling a teacher that a hammer head is loose or contacting a manufacturer when a fault is found. This is dealt with in more detail later in this section.

Introduction

A mechanism creates movement within a product - there will be occasions when you need to apply a mechanism to a product; whether it be a moving toy or a piece of serious engineering.

There are four types of movement ...

1 ROTATING
(Turning in a circle)

2 LINEAR
(Moving in one direction)

3 RECIPROCAL
(Moving backwards and forwards)

4 OSCILLATING
(Swinging in alternate directions)

General Mechanical Movement

The following theory will help you to understand how the basic elements of mechanisms work.
It is also important to look at existing products and work out what mechanisms are involved in making them move. This will help when you begin to develop your design ideas, so that you can take an existing method and build the overall design around it.

Levers 1 – Basic Principles

All machines will almost certainly have at least one lever. A lever is a simple device, consisting of a rigid bar which pivots about a fixed point. This point is called the 'fulcrum'.

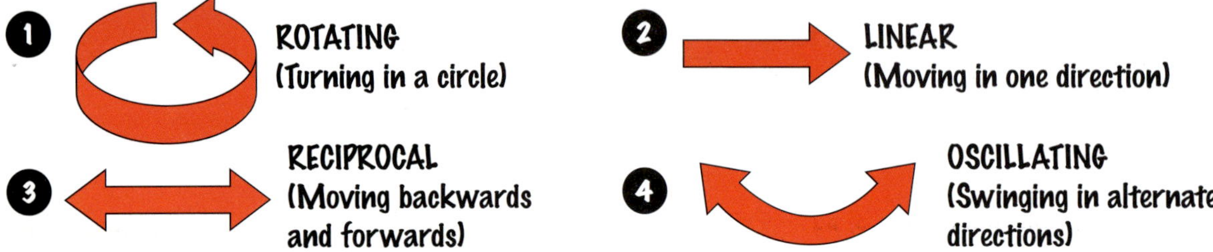

- A 'load' is applied at one end of a 'rigid bar'. The bar is placed centrally on top of the 'fulcrum' (pivot point).
- At the other end of the bar, a force is applied - called the 'effort'.
- This results in a single 'lever' movement about the pivot point.

Examples Of Levers 1

A pair of scissors is an example of a simple lever system.
- The EFFORT:- is applied by the hands at one end.
- The LOAD:- is the resistance against the cutting edge.
- The FULCRUM:- is the screw which holds the two halves together and allows for movement.

More effort is applied when cutting thicker paper or card, than when cutting thin paper.

Levers 2 – Force Multipliers

By altering the position of the fulcrum, the effort can be multiplied and therefore lift a larger load.

The leverage of the blue and yellow sections on the rigid bar, are now at a ratio of 6:2 or 3:1.

- So an effort of 1 could move a load of 3, but the effort end will have to move 3 times further than the load 'end.'

Example Of Levers 2

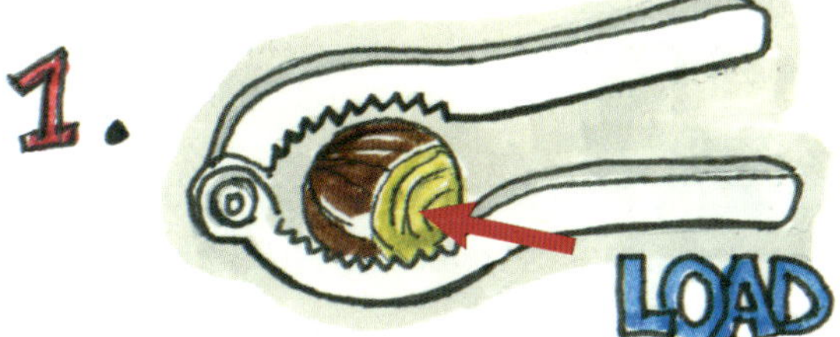

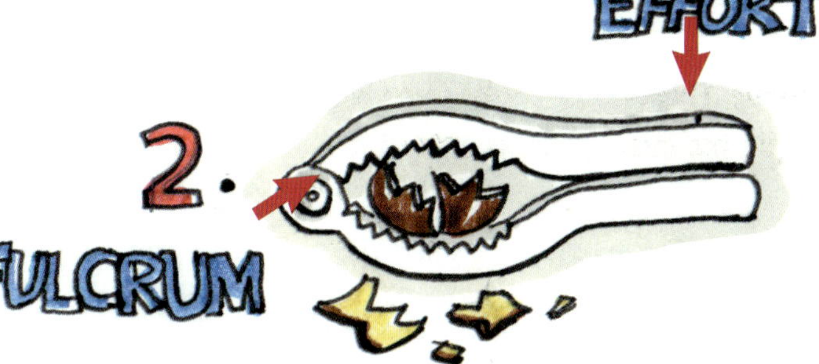

Nutcrackers are an example of how a lever can be used to act as a force multiplier. In this case, the load is closer to the fulcrum than the effort, resulting in more force being applied.

Levers 3 – Movement Multipliers

The third type of lever, is where the effort is applied between the load and the fulcrum. The effort needed is greater than the load, but this time the amount of movement is multiplied.

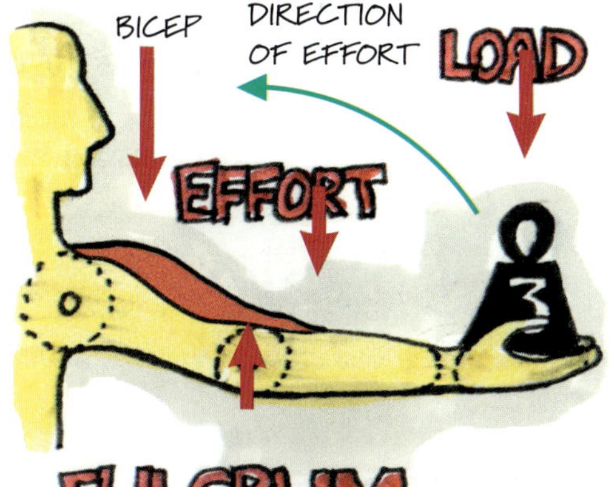

Example Of Levers 3

The elbow is the fulcrum. The effort is provided by the biceps muscle, which attaches to the forearm just below the elbow. A relatively small movement of the biceps results in a relatively large movement of the end of the lower arm, but the effort needs to be greater than the load.

Cranks and cams are relatively simple devices which convert...
... ROTARY MOTION to LINEAR MOTION (or vice versa).

Cranks

Cranks can convert linear movement to rotary movement in the case of the tricycle and child's pedal car. The crankshaft in an automobile also does this. Arranged differently, the crank can convert rotary motion to linear motion. This could be used to drive a pump for instance.

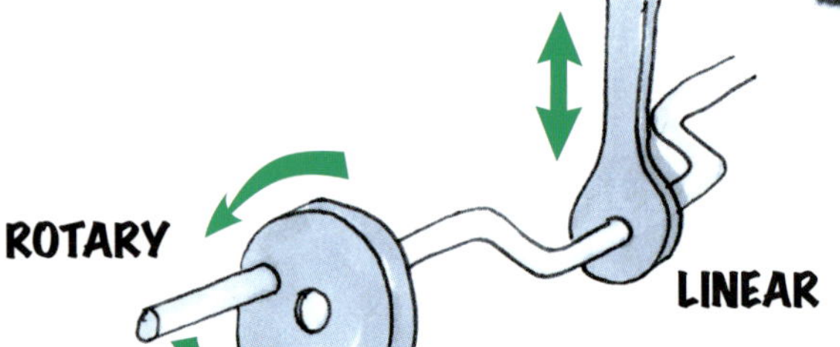

Cams

A cam is a device which converts one type of movement into another. The example below shows a ROTARY CAM which converts ROTARY MOTION into RECIPROCATING MOTION (up and down movement ↕) in the cam follower. This motion can be varied by using different shaped cams.

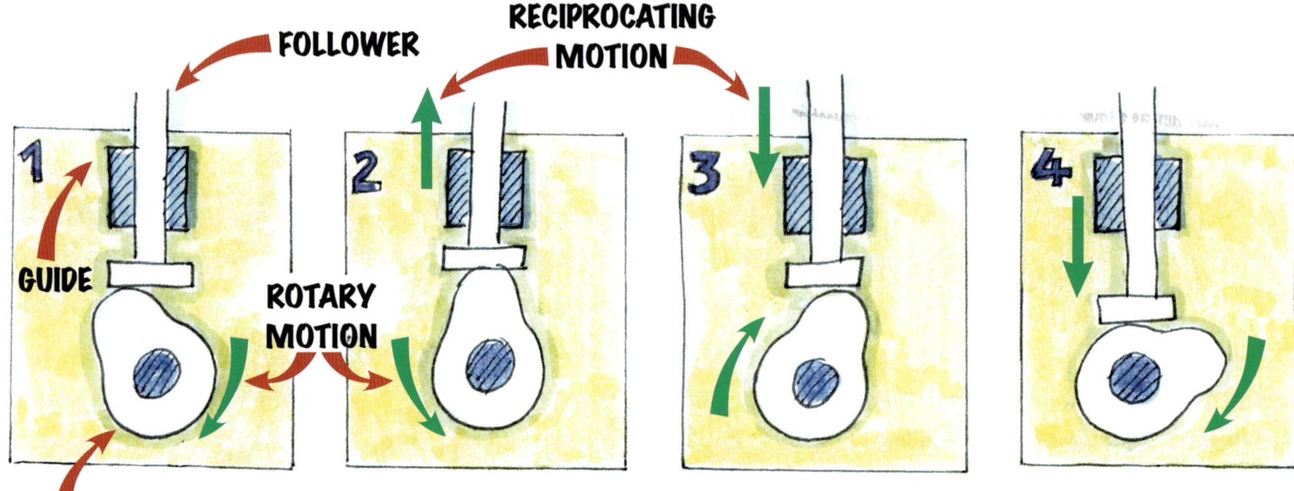

- A FOLLOWER is a rod which moves up and down. This will have an object of your choice on top.
- A GUIDE holds the FOLLOWER in place.

This is how the simple cam looks in 3D

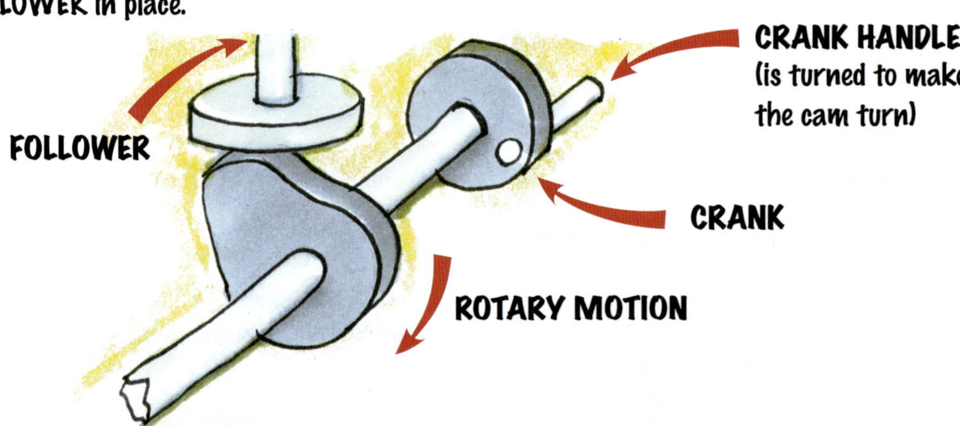

Levers 2 – Force Multipliers

By altering the position of the fulcrum, the effort can be multiplied and therefore lift a larger load.

The leverage of the blue and yellow sections on the rigid bar, are now at a ratio of 6:2 or 3:1.

- So an effort of 1 could move a load of 3, but the effort end will have to move 3 times further than the load 'end.'

Example Of Levers 2

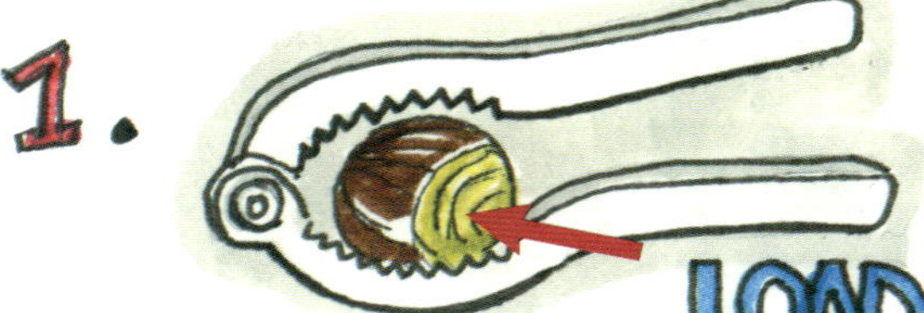

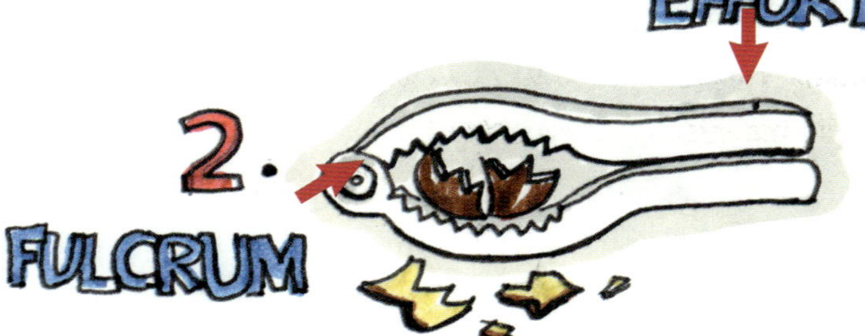

Nutcrackers are an example of how a lever can be used to act as a force multiplier.
In this case, the load is closer to the fulcrum than the effort, resulting in more force being applied.

Levers 3 – Movement Multipliers

The third type of lever, is where the effort is applied between the load and the fulcrum. The effort needed is greater than the load, but this time the amount of movement is multiplied.

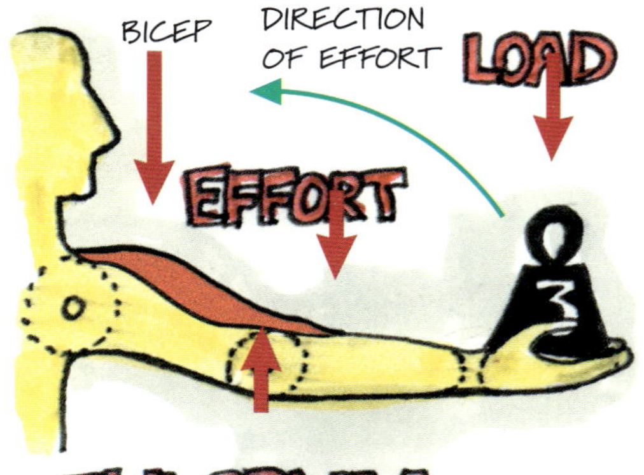

Example Of Levers 3

The elbow is the fulcrum. The effort is provided by the biceps muscle, which attaches to the forearm just below the elbow. A relatively small movement of the biceps results in a relatively large movement of the end of the lower arm, but the effort needs to be greater than the load.

Cranks and cams are relatively simple devices which convert...
... ROTARY MOTION to LINEAR MOTION (or vice versa).

Cranks

Cranks can convert linear movement to rotary movement in the case of the tricycle and child's pedal car. The crankshaft in an automobile also does this. Arranged differently, the crank can convert rotary motion to linear motion. This could be used to drive a pump for instance.

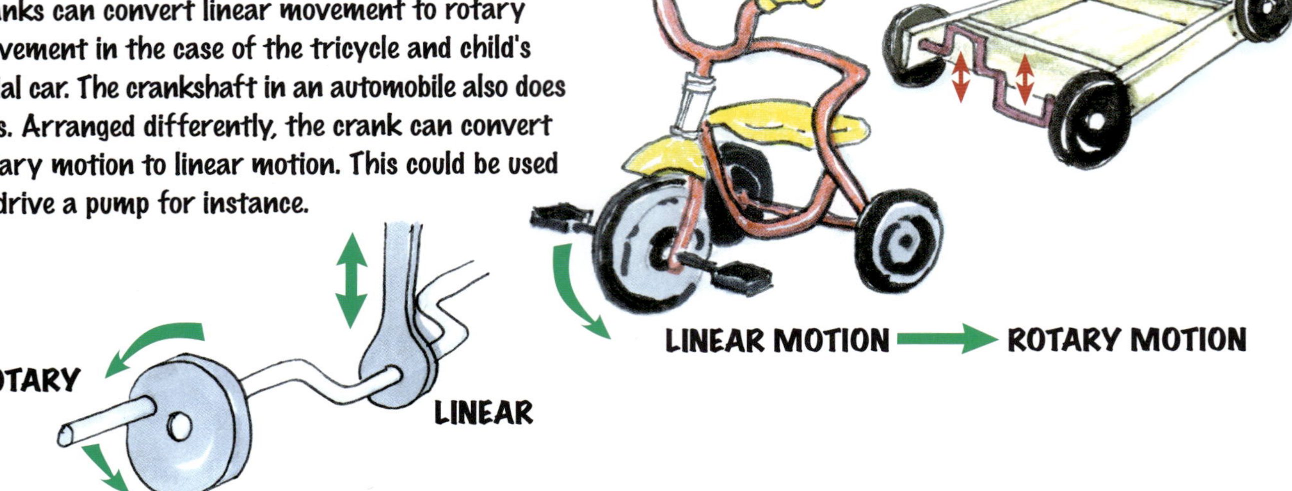

Cams

A cam is a device which converts one type of movement into another. The example below shows a ROTARY CAM which converts ROTARY MOTION into RECIPROCATING MOTION (up and down movement) in the cam follower. This motion can be varied by using different shaped cams.

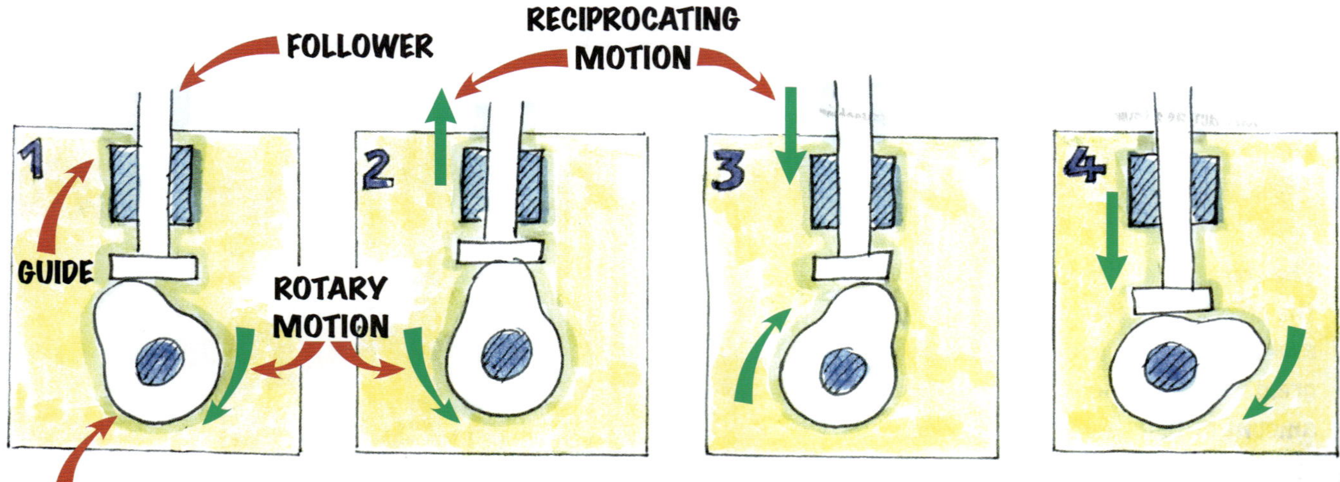

- A FOLLOWER is a rod which moves up and down. This will have an object of your choice on top.
- A GUIDE holds the FOLLOWER in place.

This is how the simple cam looks in 3D

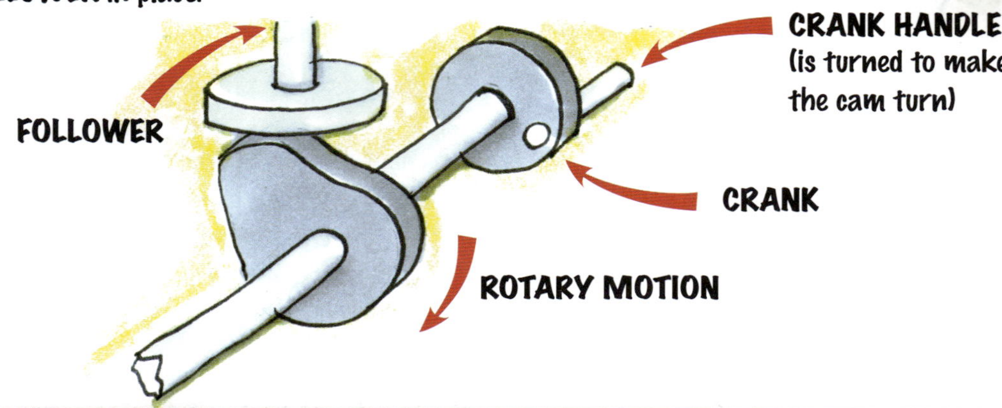

Springs

There are lots of different types of spring which are used in a variety of ways to resist different forces. They can be placed into four broad groups ...

1

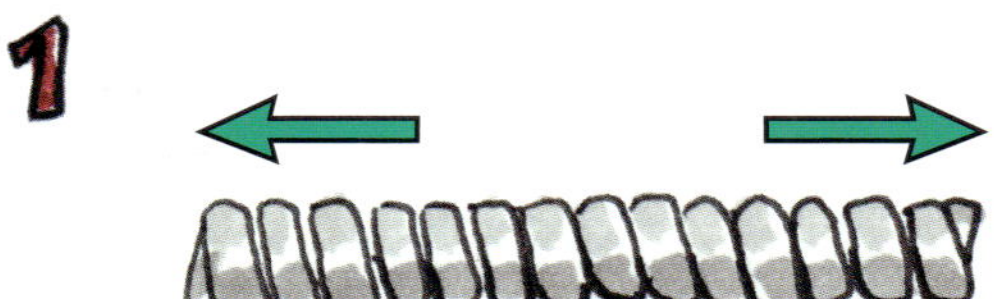

Springs which resist ...
... EXTENSION

2

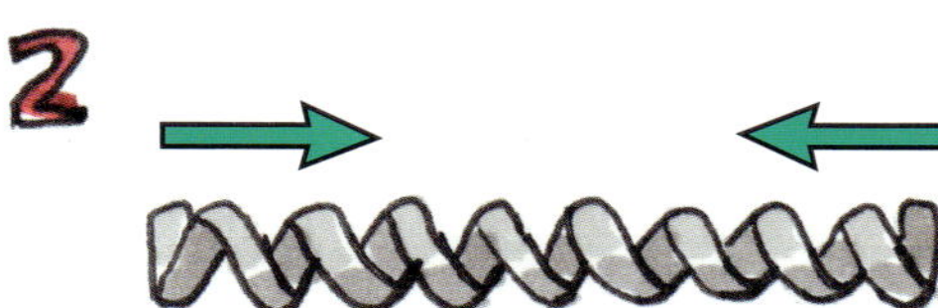

Springs which resist ...
... COMPRESSION

3

Springs which resist ...
... RADIAL MOVEMENT

4

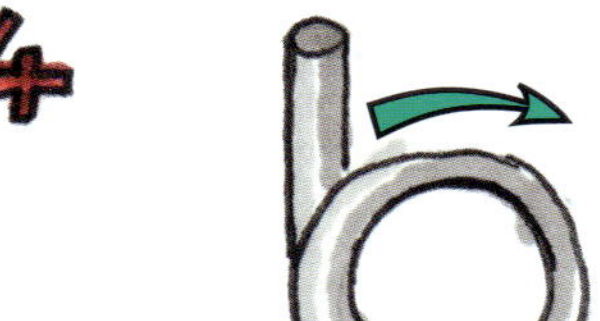

Springs which resist ...
... TWISTING

All springs resist force by trying to return to their original shape or position.

Linkages

Sometimes a linkage can act as a lever, but most times it transfers one mechanical motion to another. It is often used to connect cams to cranks or cams to levers or vice versa. Below are three simple linkage examples. A simple example, with which you may be familiar, is a metal tool box which opens to reveal different levels of trays.

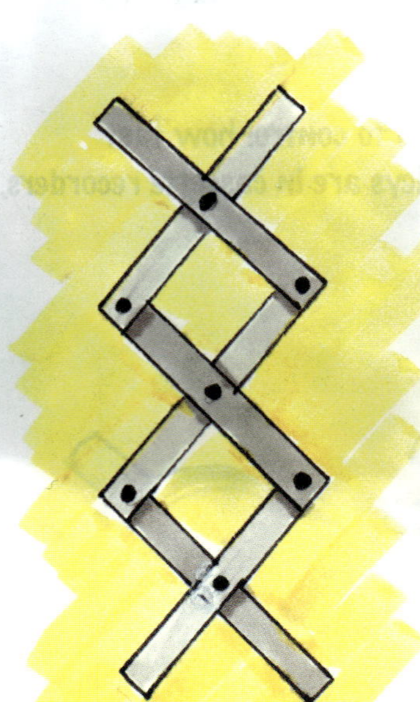

TONGS LINKAGE

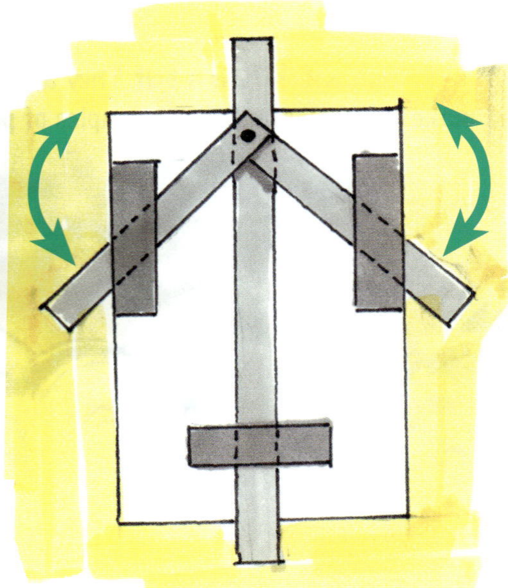

MOVING WINGS LINKAGE

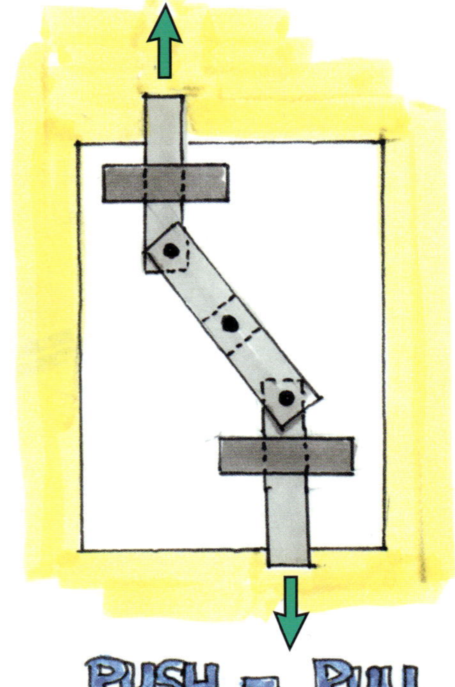

PUSH – PULL LINKAGE

Gears

Gears are like linkages, transferring one motion to another. Gear wheels have teeth around the edge which mesh with the teeth of another gear. Gear wheels may also be linked by chains or belts. Gears are used as force multipliers or reducers to make things go faster or slower. They are used on bikes and in cars; also in hand whisks, salad spinners, toys and bottle openers.

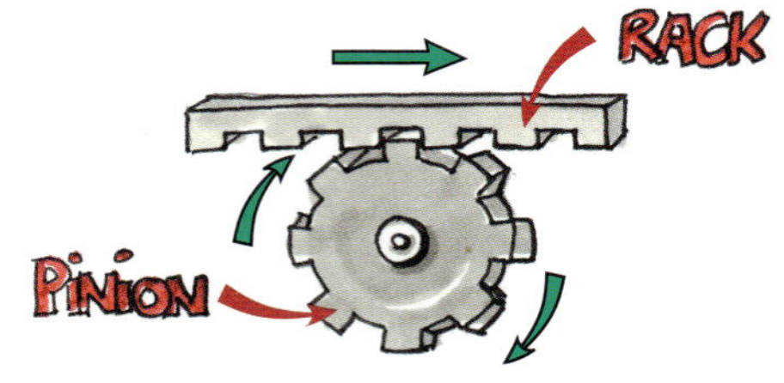

- Gears can reduce the applied force needed to cycle uphill by increasing the rate at which you have to pedal.

- A rack and pinion linkage can be used in cars to convert the rotary motion of the steering wheel into a lateral movement of the wheels.

- The pinion moves the big wheel. The big wheel has twice as many teeth therefore rotates at half the speed (but with twice the force).

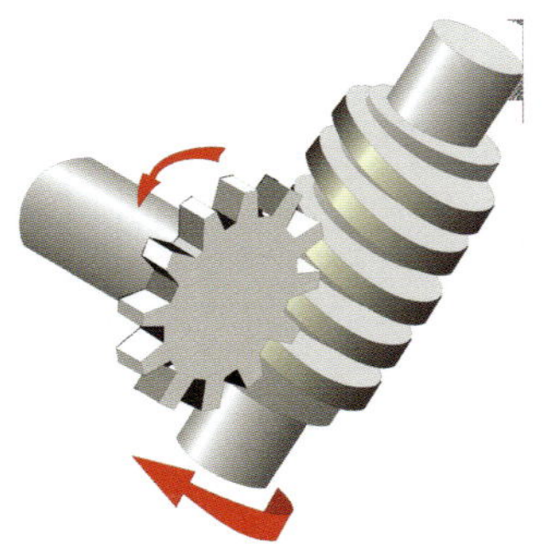

- A worm and worm wheel changes motion through 90°. The worm is usually the driver. Because of the large reduction in speed and the high torque (twisting force) this mechanism is used in products such as hand held food mixers.

- Bevel gears also change motion through 90°. If the gears are different sizes there will be a change in speed as well. They are commonly found in electric hand drills.

Pulleys

A pulley is a wheel with a groove around it through which runs a belt. They are used to control how fast something turns. Pulleys are also used to make lifting easier. Other examples of pulleys are in cassette recorders, washing machines and cranes.

1. This drive incorporates gearing - the big wheel rotates more slowly than the small wheel, but with greater force.

2. A twist in the belt (pulley) makes the wheels turn in the opposite direction.

Manufacturing

Commercial manufacturing consists of a system or group of sub-systems which require:

Special buildings or places of work.

The organisation of people.

The organisation of tools and equipment.

Information systems to help people communicate with each other reliably.

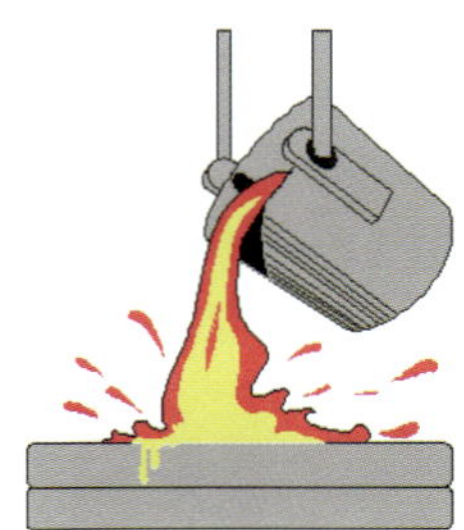

Ways of changing the shape and form of raw materials.

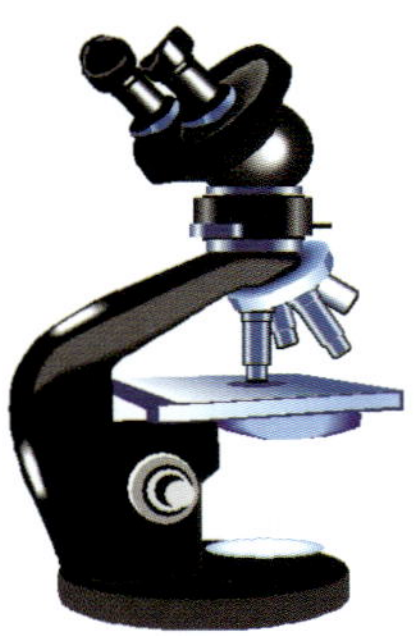

Quality Assurance procedures and quality checks to be made.

The design and production of many products in a systematic way.

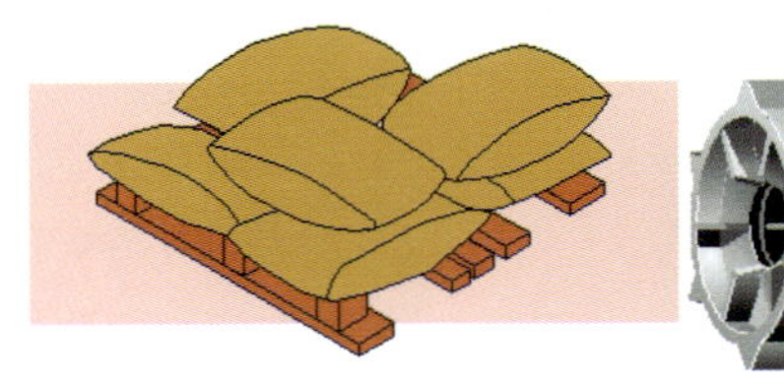

Ways of using tools and equipment to transform the materials into products.

Efficient and safe working methods.

Ways of disposing of waste in an environmentally friendly way.

Transportation of materials and finished products.

This system needs to work together regardless of the scale of production. Feedback from the workforce is essential at every stage if the aim of 'Right first time, every time' is to be achieved.

Quality Assurance

Quality Assurance checks the systems which make the products, before, during and after manufacture. It ensures that consistency is achieved and that it meets the required standards. Factors such as equipment, materials, processes and staff training need to be constantly monitored. The customer is an important part of any QA system and may well be involved in the monitoring at various stages.

Quality Control

Quality Control is a series of checks which are carried out on a product as it is made. The checks are made to make sure that each product meets a specific standard. Some likely tests carried out on the product involve ...

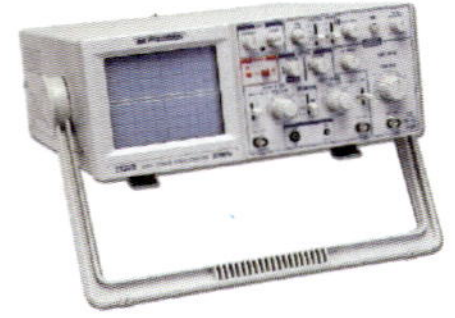

| Dimensional accuracy | Weight | Electrical circuit testing | Flammability tests |

Testing is an important part of the manufacture of a product and can take place at any time during production. For example, an injection moulded plastic bottle top could be tested after ten, a thousand or a million of them have been produced. In this particular example some of the tests would include: Checking its diameter, its thickness and whether it screws onto its container properly.

Tolerances

As every object cannot be guaranteed to accurately meet the specifications when produced in large quantities, a tolerance has to be applied. This specifies the minimum and maximum measurements. Analysis of tolerance tests can signal the imminent failure of a machine and can help to achieve the ultimate aim of quality control which is ZERO FAULTS.

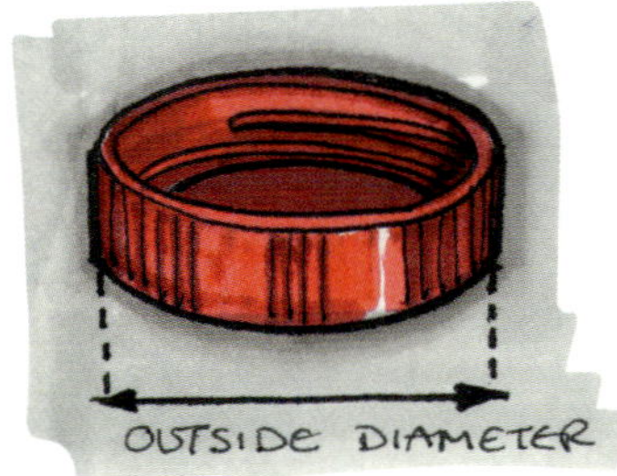

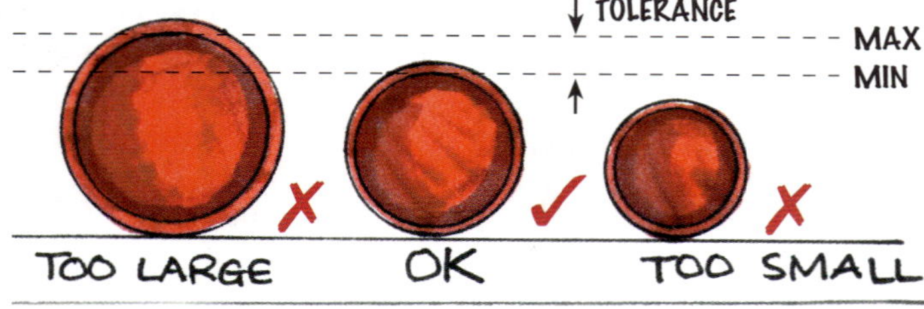

Health And Safety

Health & Safety systems are there to protect everyone. In a manufacturing environment these systems have to be continually checked and there are people who manage these. In D&T you will have a number of Health and Safety systems in place. It is vital that you know what these are as your life could depend on them.

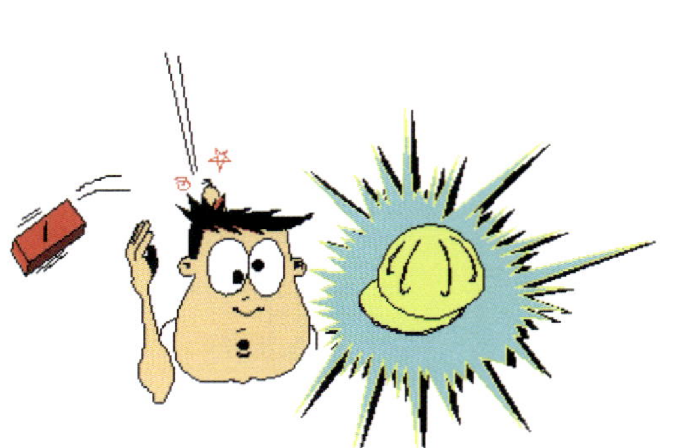
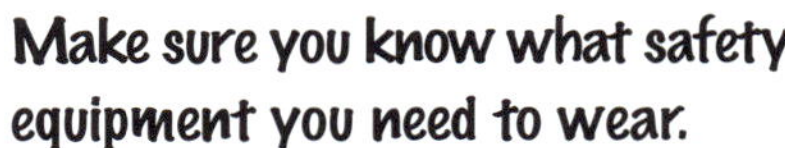

Make sure you know what safety equipment you need to wear.

Always clear away your mess. A tidy area is a safer one.

Do you know where to put the waste? Many materials need to be disposed of very carefully to reduce risk of fire or environmental problems.

Don't lift heavy items. It may seem cool but can be very dangerous.

Check out fire procedures. Do you know what the different extinguishers are for? Do you know where the fire exits are?

Do you know what to do if there is an accident? Who do you tell?

Risk Assessment

Risk assessment is a system for looking at the likelihood of problems arising from every activity. Your teachers will have done a risk assessment for every machine and for every process in D&T. Try doing your own risk assessment for your product.

What Health & Safety warnings might you have to provide with the product you design and make?

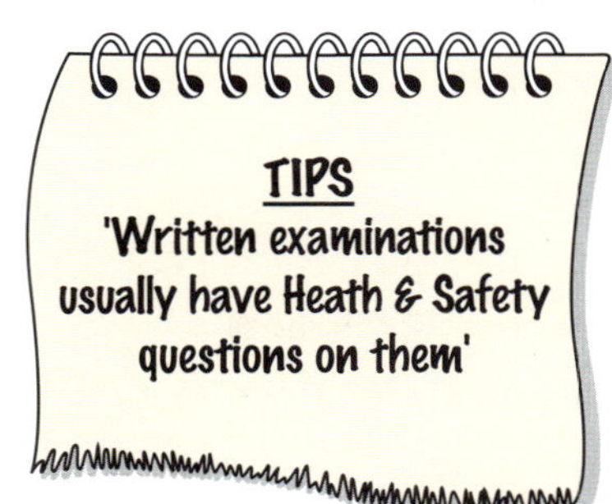

A
Abrading 62, 63
Abrasive Cloth 62
Abrasive Papers 62
Acrylic 50
Adhesives 77
Aluminium 47
Analysis 16
Anodising 81
Anthropometrics 12, 14
AQA 4
Art CAM 39
Art Deco 20
Art Nouveau 20
Ash 42

B
Bauhaus 20
Beech 42
Bevels 53
Blockboard 41, 44
Bolts 75
Brass 48

C
CAD 26, 39
Calipers 78
   Odd-leg 53
CAM 40
Camera 8, 38
Cams 86
Card Templates 53
Cast Iron 46
Casting 67
Casting Alloy 48
CD ROMS 39
Cedar
   Western Red 43
   Yellow 43
Centre Lathe 61
Centre Punch 53e
Checking 78, 79
Chipboard 41, 44
Chisels 57
Circles, Drawing Of 35
Clamps 54
CNC Milling 60
CNC Turning 61
Compasses 8
Computers 9, 38
Conductive Polymers 52
Copper 47
Crating Out 32
Cramps 54
Cranks 86
Cutters 38

D
Databases 16, 17
De Stijl 20
Decision 25
Design
   Brief 7
   Folder 6, 10
   Proposal 7, 27
Designers 21
Desktop Publishing 38
Development 23
Die Casting 68
Dimensioning 36
Duralumin 48
Dividers 53
Drawing board 8
Drills 59
Dyson 21

E
Edexcel 4
Electronic Product Definition 26
Epoxy Resin 51
Equipment 8
Eraser 8
Ergonome 12, 13
Ergonomics 12, 16
Evaluation 23, 28, 29, 30
Examiner's Advice 5

Exploded Drawings 35
Exploded Drawings 35
Extrusion 69

F
Felt Tip Pens 8
Files 62
Fineline Pen 8
Fixtures 55
Flexible Curves 9
Flow Charts 25
Forging 66
French Curves 9
French Polish 80
Functions 15

G
Galvanising 81
Gap Gauge 79
Gears 88
Graphics 38
Grids 21
Guilding Metal 48

H
Hammers 64
Hardwood 41, 44

I
ICT 38
Ideas 20, 22, 23
Input 25
Internet 39
Interviews 16
Isometric Projection 34, 35

J
Jelutang 42
Jigs 54
Joints 72, 73

K
Knock-down Fittings 73

L
Lacquers 80
Laminboard 41
Lasers 79
Lathes 76
Lead 47
Lenticular Polypropylene Sheet 52
Levers 84, 85
Line Bending 71
Lines 36
Linkages 87
Lost Pattern Casting 67

M
Mackintosh 21
Mahogany 42
Mallets 64
Manufactured Boards 41, 44
Manufacturing 16, 89
Marking Gauge 53
Materials 16, 17
   Bending Of 65
   Forging Of 66
   Cutting Of 65
MDF 41, 44
Measuring 78, 79
   Stick 79
Melamine Formaldehyde 51
Memphis 20
Metals 45
   Alloys 45, 48
   Ferrous 45, 46
   Non-ferrous 45, 47
   Properties Of 45
Micrometer 78
Milling 60
Modelling 21, 22, 24, 27
Moderators 6
Modifications 30
Monomers 40
Motion 86
Moulding
   Blow 70

Compression 70
   Injection 69
   Rotational 71
Multi-axis Machines 40

N
Nails 73
Nichrome Wire 52
Nuts 75
Nylon 50

O
Oak 42
OCR 4
Oil 80
Opinions 23
Output 25

P
Pencils 8
People 11
Pewter 48
Phenol Formaldehyde 51
Pine
   Parane 43
   Scots 43
Places 11
Planes 58
Planing 58
Plans 25
Plastic Dip-coating 81
Plastics 49
Plating 812
Plotters 38
Plywood 41, 44
Points 80
Polishing 82
Polyester Resin 51
Polymers 49
Polymorph 52
Polypropylene 50
Polystyrene 50
Polythene 50
Powder Coating 81
Presentation Drawings 27
Pressing 65
Pro/DESKTOP 27, 39
Process 25
Processes 11
Production 30, 31
   Batch 31
   Continuos 31
   Just In Time 31
   Mass 31
   One-off 31
Products 11
Project 26
Prototype 28
Prototyping 40
Protractor 8
Pulleys 88
PVC 50

Q
Quality
   Assurance 90
   Control 90
Questionnaires 16

R
Rendering 33
Research 18
Revision 5
Risk Assessment 91
Rivets 75
Routing 60
Ruler 8

S
Sanders
   Belt 63
   Hand-held 63
Sanding
   Disc 63
   Sealer 81
   Rotary 63

Machines 63
Saws 56
Scale 24, 36
Scanners 38
Screw Cutting 75
Screws 73

Scriber 53
Self-finishes 81
Set Square 8
Shaker 20
Sketching 32
Smart Materials 52
Softwood 41, 43
Soldering 74
Sottsass 21
Specifications 4, 5, 7, 9
Spirit Level 78
Split Pattern Sand Casting 67
Spokeshave 58
Spreadsheets 16, 38
Springs 87
Spruce 43
Stark 21
Steel
   High Speed 46
   Mild 46
   Stainless 46
   Tool 46
   Rule 78
Styles 16, 20
Surform 58
Systems
   Health And Safety 83, 91
   Mechanical 83
   Production 83, 89
   Quality Assurance 83, 90

T
T-square 8
Tape Measure 9, 78
Tapping 76
Teak 42
Templates
   Circle 9
   Ellipse 9
Terminator 24
Testing 19, 24, 29
   Materials 17
Texture 33
Thermoplastics 40, 50
Thermosetting Plastics 49, 51
Thermocolour Sheet 52
Third Angle Orthographic Projection 36, 37
Threading 76
Timber 41
   Joining Of 72, 73
Time-plan 10
Tin 47
Tolerances 90
Tone 33
Try Square 53, 79
Turning 61

U
Ultrasonics 79
Urea Formaldehyde 51

V
Vacuum Forming 71
Varnishes 80
Vernier Gauge 78
Vices 54

W
Welding 74
Wood Stains 81
Wood-turning Lathe 61
Work-plan 6, 7
Working Drawings 36
Wright 21

Z
Zinc 47